Australian Mythology

Captivating Dreamtime Stories of Indigenous Australians

© **Copyright 2020**

All Rights Reserved. No part of this book may be reproduced in any form without permission in writing from the author. Reviewers may quote brief passages in reviews.

Disclaimer: No part of this publication may be reproduced or transmitted in any form or by any means, mechanical or electronic, including photocopying or recording, or by any information storage and retrieval system, or transmitted by email without permission in writing from the publisher.

While all attempts have been made to verify the information provided in this publication, neither the author nor the publisher assumes any responsibility for errors, omissions or contrary interpretations of the subject matter herein.

This book is for entertainment purposes only. The views expressed are those of the author alone, and should not be taken as expert instruction or commands. The reader is responsible for his or her own actions.

Adherence to all applicable laws and regulations, including international, federal, state and local laws governing professional licensing, business practices, advertising and all other aspects of doing business in the US, Canada, UK or any other jurisdiction is the sole responsibility of the purchaser or reader.

Neither the author nor the publisher assumes any responsibility or liability whatsoever on the behalf of the purchaser or reader of these materials. Any perceived slight of any individual or organization is purely unintentional.

Free Bonus from Captivating History (Available for a Limited time)

Hi History Lovers!

Now you have a chance to join our exclusive history list so you can get your first history ebook for free as well as discounts and a potential to get more history books for free! Simply visit the link below to join.

Captivatinghistory.com/ebook

Also, make sure to follow us on Facebook, Twitter and Youtube by searching for Captivating History.

Indigenous reader advice: Aboriginal and Torres Strait Islander readers are advised that this text may contain the names of people who have passed away.

Contents

INTRODUCTION 1
PART I: ORIGINS 4
PART II: GODS, HEROES, AND MONSTERS 26
PART III: ANIMAL TALES 61
BIBLIOGRAPHY 84

Introduction

With a history reaching back over 40,000 years, Indigenous Australian culture is one of the oldest continually existing cultures in the world. According to DNA tests conducted at the University of Copenhagen, Indigenous Australian people are the descendants of the first migrants to have left the birthplace of humanity in Africa, some 75,000 years ago. Across these many millennia, the Indigenous peoples of Australia have established complex and unique societies that have adapted well to the often harsh conditions of the Australian landscape.

Although Indigenous Australian culture tends to be named as though it were a single unit, it is far from monolithic. According to the Australian government's website, at the time of first contact with Europeans, there were some 500 distinct Indigenous nations inhabiting Australia, speaking different languages and following their own religious and cultural practices, with a certain amount of overlap across cultures.

As with all human societies, that of the Indigenous Australians is abounding in stories. Stories of how the world came to be the way it is, stories of heroism and perfidy, stories about animals and birds, and stories about love and hate all have parts to play in the wide array of myths, legends, and tales created by Indigenous Australians.

One of the most important concepts connected to Indigenous Australian mythmaking and storytelling is that of the Dreamtime. "Dreamtime" refers to the Indigenous mythic past, the time of the ancestors when the world was newly made and animals and birds lived and talked like people. It also refers to aspects of current Indigenous religious practices and beliefs. As anthropologist Diane James reports, for Indigenous peoples, the Dreamtime does not exist as something separate in history from their world today. In fact, for them it never really ended, and thus past and present exist together in a kind of unbroken continuum.

This volume is devoted to stories that Indigenous Australians tell about the Dreamtime and is comprised of three parts. The first deals with the origins of things and how the world came to be; the second tells stories of gods, heroes, and monsters; and the third presents tales about animals and birds.

Although there are some aspects of Australian creation myths that span the continent (such as the character of the Rainbow Serpent), different tribes generally have different gods and thus differing stories about the creation of the universe. For tribes in the state of Victoria, the knife-wielding Pundjel is the creator-god, while in other parts of southern Australia, Baiame creates the world with the help of Yhi, the Sun Goddess. Some of these stories address the creation of the world as a whole, while others deal with certain features, such as how the Pleiades and the Morning Star came to be or how Uluru (Ayers Rock) came to have the markings it does.

The Dreamtime is also home to heroes and monsters, deeds of strength and valor, and perilous journeys to the very ends of the earth. In the Dreamtime, the gods still walked among humankind, and their doings at that time are the subject of several myths. Indigenous Australian myths also tell of the deeds of the semi-divine Winjarning Brothers, who travel wherever their courage, skill, and strength are needed. Yet other stories tell of the bravery of ordinary people who save their loved ones from vile beasts or who travel through many strange lands full of even stranger creatures to arrive at Kurrilwan, the land beyond the sunset, where Baiame lives still.

Animal tales are the backbone of many storytelling traditions, and thus the third section of this book presents a selection of Dreamtime animal stories. In these myths, creatures are animal and human at the same time, having feathers, fur, and tails but also paddling canoes, hunting with spears, and speaking and acting like people. Some of these tales are just-so stories explaining why some animals have certain characteristics, while others explain how the animal or bird we know today was created out of its Dreamtime human form.

As of this writing, climate change has generated conditions for catastrophic bushfires that have burned almost fifteen million acres along Australia's southeast coast, with no sign of the fires abating. The precious birds, animals, and plants that inspired so many of these stories and that are often unique to this island continent are in serious jeopardy, as are the homes, lives, and livelihoods of thousands of human beings who call that part of the world their home. Written works can always preserve the stories of Indigenous Australians for future generations, especially with our current ability to host texts in the Cloud as well as in printed books, but the fate of Australia's land, creatures, and peoples are not as well assured. We can only hope that the things that make Australia and her peoples wonderful and unique will continue to exist in physical reality and not just as words and images in tales from the Dreamtime.

Part I: Origins

The Creation of Life

The responsibility for the creation of the world varies within the corpus of Australian myth. In some myths, the creator is the Rainbow Serpent, while in others it is the god Baiame. In the myth retold below, Baiame passes the responsibility for creating life to Yhi, the Sun Goddess, who is not herself created but exists in a kind of suspended animation until awoken by Baiame. Except for the plants, which Yhi calls into existence by walking across a barren world, all living things are brought forth from caves under the ground.

In some versions of the myth, Yhi's act of creation is located on the Nullarbor Plain, which is located along the coast of the state of South Australia and extends across the border into Western Australia. The plain's name is a colonialist creation, compounded out of "nulla," and "arbor," which are the Latin words for "none" and "tree," respectively. This name was given to the area by Westerners because there are very few trees at all there.

At the very beginning of the world, everything lay under a blanket of darkness. Darkness enveloped the plains and the mountains. Nothing stirred, nothing moved, not even the tiniest breath of wind. There was no sound and no light, only darkness and silence and waiting.

In a place far, far beyond the Earth, Yhi slept. The Sun Goddess slept in the darkness. Like the Earth, she waited in darkness and silence.

Out of the darkness and silence came Baiame. He went to Yhi and whispered in her ear. "Yhi! Awake! The world is ready to have life. You must wake!"

Yhi heard the whisper of Baiame, and she awoke. When she opened her eyes, the whole world was flooded with light. Yhi could see the mountains and the plains, and her breath stirred the still air, making the first breezes blow.

Yhi began her walk on the Nullarbor Plain, and wherever she went, plants of all kinds began to grow. As she walked, grasses and flowers, trees and shrubs all sprang up, and soon the plains and the mountains were full of green and growing things, and many-colored flowers glowed among the greenery.

When plants of all kinds were growing everywhere, Yhi rested. And after she had been resting for a while, Baiame again spoke to her. "Yhi! The world needs yet more life! Go under the earth. Go deep into the caverns under the ground and see what life may be created there."

Yhi heeded the call of Baiame. She went into the caverns under the earth. The spirits who lived there cried out at the flood of light Yhi brought into their domain. "Why are you here?" they cried. "Leave us in peace! Leave us our darkness, and let us sleep!"

The voices of the underground spirits did not deter Yhi. She walked through all the underground caverns, and wherever she went, a myriad of insects came forth. Creeping insects, flying insects, insects with many-colored bodies and many-colored wings all came skittering and chittering out of the darkness of the caves. Then they went above ground to live among the plants that Yhi had created.

When Yhi was done calling forth the insects, she left the caverns beneath the ground, leaving the spirits to their darkness, and then she went home and rested for a time.

After her rest, Yhi again went forth. She went into another deep, dark cave, one that was full of ice. Yhi's warmth and light melted the ice, and from this cave came snakes and lizards that slithered and crawled up to the surface to live among the plants and insects there. The melted ice flowed out of the cave in a mighty rush. It became a river, flowing peacefully across the land, and the river was full of all manner of fish.

When Yhi saw that the snakes and lizards and fish were settled in their new homes, she went back into the cavern again. The reptiles and insects watched her create yet more life. In this cavern, Yhi found things with feathers and things with fur. Soon birds of all kinds were flying out of the cavern to join Yhi's other creatures, and animals of all kinds ran out into the new world with them.

Baiame looked at all that Yhi had created and was pleased. "You have brought life to my world," he said. "Everything you have made is very, very good."

Yhi then gathered all the living things together and explained that there would be different seasons. There would be seasons that were colder and seasons that were hotter, and they would follow one another by turns. She also explained that soon light and darkness would follow one another just s hot and cold would.

Yhi said to her creations, "My work here is done. I must go and live in the sky now. I will still give you light and warmth and life, but I must do it from far away."

Then Yhi rose up into the sky, where she became a bright ball of light. She went into the western sky, where she began to walk down toward the horizon. As she walked down, her color changed, and her light began to dim. Soon Yhi had gone all the way down below the horizon, and darkness fell upon the earth. All the creatures were afraid. "Yhi, come back!" they cried. "Do not leave us here in the darkness!"

The creatures need not have worried. After a period of darkness, the eastern horizon began to glow with light. It was Yhi, who was returning to look upon her creation. She rose up above the land and began her walk across the sky as the birds sang welcoming songs to the dawn. Now the world had both day and night, and the days and nights could be counted.

When Yhi sank down below the horizon at the end of that first day, the creatures were again dismayed. Yhi heard their distress and took pity on them. Yhi made the Morning Star and sent Bahloo, the Moon, to live in the sky with the Morning Star as her husband. And so the Morning Star and the Moon shine when Yhi has gone to her rest so that the creatures know that Yhi cares for them and will return at the start of a new day.

Pundjel the Creator

Pundjel is a creator-god revered by Indigenous peoples in the state of Victoria. One of his distinguishing characteristics is the large knife that he carries with him, with which he does some of his work of creation. Pundjel is not alone in creating the world, however. He has a brother named Pallyan, who discovers the first women in the mud of a pond.

As with the myths of many cultures around the world, those concerning Pundjel also explain the problem of good and evil and how the coming of evil affects the structure of the universe. Here, the wicked do not suffer death but rather are removed from the place where they were living and then scattered throughout the broader world.

Pundjel it was who created the whole world. And when the world was made, Pundjel thought that it might be good to make some people to live in it. He thought for a while about how he might go about doing this, and when his plan was made, he took his big knife and went out looking for some tree bark. When he found some bark of the right kind, he cut some off the tree. Then he went looking for some clay. Soon he found all the clay he needed.

When Pundjel had all the things he needed to make people, he took some of the clay and put it into one piece of the bark. He worked the clay until it was just the right consistency. Then he split the clay into two pieces and put one piece of clay into each piece of bark. Pundjel began to shape each bit of clay into a man. He started by making the feet, then the legs, then the body. Pundjel kept working until his clay men were completely formed.

Once the men were made, Pundjel looked at them and saw that they were very good. Pundjel put the pieces of bark that held the clay men in them onto the ground, and he danced all around them.

Pundjel then looked again at the men he had made and saw that they needed hair. So he went and cut some bark from a different tree and made it into hair for the clay men. To one man he gave straight hair, and to the other he gave curly hair. This also was very good, and it delighted Pundjel so much that he danced around the clay men once again.

When that was done, Pundjel again went over the bodies and made sure that the clay was in just the right shape to be a man. Then he went and breathed into each clay figure, first into their mouths, then into their noses, then into their navels. He breathed very hard into the clay men, and they came alive and took breaths of their own. Pundjel saw that the clay men had become living creatures, and so he danced around them again. Then Pundjel gave each man the ability to move and taught them how to speak, and that was how the first men were made, back in the Dreamtime.

Now, Pundjel had a brother named Pallyan, and Pallyan was the ruler over all the waters. He liked nothing better than to wade in the streams and in the surf or to dive down to the bottom of lakes and of the ocean. One day, Pallyan was paddling about in a pond and delighting in the movement and sound of the water, and his play stirred up a great quantity of mud. Soon the mud was so thick in the water that Pallyan could no longer see through it.

Even with the thickness of the mud in the water, Pallyan caught a glimpse of something as he continued his play. He looked closer and saw what looked a bit like the hand of one of the men Pundjel had made. Pallyan made a hook out of a twig and fished about in the water. He pushed the water aside and saw that there were two figures in the mud of the pond. They looked almost the same as the men Pundjel had made. They had heads and arms, bodies and legs, but they weren't exactly like Pundjel's clay men. Pallyan had found the first women, who had been made by his play in the waters of the pond.

Pallyan brought the women to Pundjel, who was very pleased with them. He gave one woman to each man and then began to teach them how to live. Pundjel gave each man a spear, and to each woman he gave a digging stick. He taught the men how to hunt and the women how to dig for yams and other good things to eat.

Pundjel and Pallyan taught the women and men how to live for three more days. At the end of the third day, they all sat down together, and when they were seated, a great wind blew up. The wind blew and blew, and a great storm began. The wind and the storm took Pundjel and Pallyan away up into the heavens, and that is where they stayed.

Now, after Pundjel and Pallyan went away, the men and women lived together and had many children. And their children had children, and their grandchildren had children, and soon there were many people indeed. For a long time, the people lived well and behaved well, but there came a time when many of the people became wicked and delighted in doing bad things. Pundjel saw what the wicked people were doing, and it made him very angry.

Pundjel went down to the Earth and caused a great whirlwind to blow. The wind blew and blew, and as it blew, Pundjel went among the wicked people with his big knife and cut the people into little pieces. As each piece hit the ground, it began to writhe the way a worm does. Once all the bad people had been cut into pieces, the whirlwind picked them up and blew them away. Pundjel made the wind blow all the pieces far away and drop them in places all over the world. The people who had been good Pundjel picked up and placed in the heavens, where they became stars. And this is how the whole world came to have people in it and how the sky came to have stars.

The Wawilak Sisters

The Rainbow Serpent appears as a creator-being in myths across many Australian cultures. The cycle of myths that contains the story of the Wawilak Sisters combines the creative force of the Rainbow Serpent with that of the Djanggawul, a brother and two sisters who are revered by the Yolngu people of Arnhem Land in the Northern Territory as creators of the landscape and plants of Australia, as well as the ancestors of the people of the Dua clans.

By the time the story of the Wawilak Sisters takes place, the world has already been made and peopled. The sisters' act of creation is located instead in the names of the plants, animals, and places that the sisters discover on their travels and also in their gift of songs, dances, and ceremonies to the Dua clans, whose totem is the serpent.

Long, long ago, far back in the Dreamtime, Yurlunggur the Rainbow Serpent created the world. And when he was done creating, he went to dwell at the bottom of a deep water hole in the place where the Liagalawumiri people live. That water hole is filled by springs that come from the very center of the Earth itself. All around the hole, there were many plants and animals, although in those days they looked and moved and lived like people, while in the waters with Yurlunggur there dwelt many different kinds of spirits.

There were no people yet, far back in the Dreamtime, until a brother and his sisters came in a canoe to the eastern shore of the land. They had fled their own country because the brother had slept with his sisters, which was a crime in the eyes of Yurlunggur. The descendants of the brother and the sisters settled along the coast, moving southward as their families grew and flourished.

Now, among these descendants were two sisters, named Garangal and Boalere. Garangal had a small baby, but Boalere had not yet found a man she liked well enough to give her a child of her own. The sisters lived peacefully and well with their people, gathering food and water, as well as giving names to the creatures and plants they found in the land about them.

One day, a man approached Boalere and said, "I would like to talk to you. Will you come with me?" Boalere wasn't sure she wanted to go with him. In their tribe, Boalere and the man were considered relatives of a sort because they had the same totem. If it turned out he wanted to lie with her, they would be committing incest, and that would bring about grave consequences.

For many days, the man persisted. For many days, Boalere looked upon him, not knowing what she wanted to do. But she did know that he was handsome and kind, so finally she gave in and went into the bush with him. Many days passed. Boalere realized that she was with child. She told her sister what she had done, and Garangal said, "Oh, no! We mustn't stay here. If people find out what you did, they will punish you! We need to leave at once."

Boalere knew her sister was right. She agreed to leave with Garangal as soon as everyone else was asleep. In the dead of night, Garangal wrapped her son warmly in paper bark, then the women gathered up their things and slipped into the bush and headed to the north, without telling anyone where they were going or why.

Traveling turned out to be a very pleasant adventure. The women saw many new lands and many new plants, birds, and animals. They gave names to every one of these. They found plenty of food and water, and they rested often because Garangal had to stop and nurse her son when he got hungry.

Finally, the women arrived at the water hole where Yurlunggur lived. They stopped to make camp like they always had, but Boalere knew something was different. Her belly had grown and grown during her travels with her sister, and now she knew that the child would soon be born. When Boalere's pains began, Garangal helped her. After much effort, Boalere delivered a beautiful boy.

Knowing that Boalere needed to rest, Garangal went out into the bush to find food. She caught a bandicoot and some grubs, and when she returned to the camp, she made a fire and began to cook a meal. But no sooner had the bandicoot been placed over the fire to cook than it came back to life and went running to the water hole, where it jumped in and disappeared below the surface.

Garangal thought this very strange, but she knew there were still the grubs to be eaten. But when she turned to her dilly bag to get them out, she saw them inching along in a line, making straight for the water just as the bandicoot had done. Instead of trying to recapture the grubs, Garangal watched them until they reached the water, where they jumped in and disappeared below the surface.

"Well, those were all animals," said Garangal to herself. "I can always cook some plants. Those won't go anywhere."

Garangal got out the yams she had collected and began to cook them. But no sooner had the heat of the fire touched the skins of the yams than they, too, went wriggling away and then dove into the watering hole, just as the bandicoot and the grubs had done.

"That was very odd indeed," thought Garangal. "I wonder what would happen if I gathered some paper bark? Boalere will need it to wrap her child in."

Garangal went to the water hole. She got into the lovely, clear water and began to swim to the other side where there were many paper bark trees. Unbeknownst to Garangal, she had started her time of the month, and some of her menstrual blood mixed with the water as she swam along.

Now, the water here was also the home of Yurlunggur, and he had awakened when he heard the voices of the women and the cries of their babies. He didn't think too much of it at first, but when he smelled Garangal's blood, he became very angry that she had fouled his pool in that way. He rose up out of the pool, taking a great mouthful of the tainted water as he went. When he broke the surface, he stretched his body up toward the sky, and he spat out the mouthful of water. The water turned into rain clouds, and soon a great torrent of rain began to fall.

The women watched in horror as the great serpent stretched its length high above them, and they scrambled to make a shelter for themselves and their babies as the rain came down.

"This is no ordinary storm," said Boalere. "I will sing to make it stop."

Boalere took her singing sticks and went out into the pouring rain. She began singing her power song and dancing her sacred dance. But no matter how well she sang and how well she danced, she could do nothing to stop the rain. Moreover, dancing and singing so soon after giving birth made Boalere bleed again, and Yurlunggur smelled that blood, too. Enraged, the huge snake coiled itself around the women's camp. It paused a moment and listened to the words of Boalere's song, a power song of the people of the serpent totem. Yurlunggur knew that it would be wrong to harm the women and their children because they had the same totem as himself, but he was so angry that he ignored that important custom. He pushed aside the women's shelter, then swallowed the babies and their mothers whole. Then he stretched his body up toward the sky once more.

Other totemic serpents saw Yurlunggur stretching himself up toward the sky. They decided to join him and ask what he had been doing.

One serpent said, "Is it you that made this rain, Yurlunggur?"

"Yes, indeed it is I that made this rain," replied the great serpent.

Then another snake noticed that Yurlunggur's body was distended from having eaten the women and their babies.

"What have you been eating?" asked the snake.

"Oh, nothing really," said Yurlunggur, who was now feeling guilty that he had violated an important custom and was worrying about what the other snakes would say.

"That's an awfully large nothing," said a third snake. "Come now, tell us the truth. What did you eat?"

Yurlunggur hesitated. Yet another snake insisted that he tell them what he had eaten. Finally, after all the snakes had demanded that Yurlunggur tell them what was in his belly, the great snake said, "Fine, I'll tell you. I ate those women and their babies, the ones that were camped near my water hole."

The other snakes stared at Yurlunggur, disgusted.

"You ate your own sisters? And your own sisters' children? How could you do such a thing?" said the first snake who had spoken.

"Yes," said the other snakes. "How could you do that? You yourself made it a law that totemic serpents must not eat the serpent people, but you ate both the women, and their children besides!"

Angry and ashamed, Yurlunggur crashed his great body back down to the earth. Now, some say that he vomited up the women and their children right then and there, while others say he spat the women out in a different place where they turned to stones, while keeping the children in his belly. But all agree that the women sent dreams to the wise men of their tribe, dreams that told their story and explained the songs, dances, and ceremonies that must be done in their honor. And this is how Garangal and Boalere gave important knowledge to the Serpent People.

How the Sun Was Made

In her collection of Australian legends, author Katie Langloh Parker states that the version of this myth told to her belonged to the Noongaburrah (Ngyiampaa) people of New South Wales. Here, the sun is not a divine being but rather is created as an unintended consequence of an argument between Dinewan, the emu, and

Bralgah, the crane. This tale also functions as a just-so story explaining why kookaburras make their laughing calls at daybreak.

At the beginning of the world, there were only the moon and the stars in the sky. The moon and the stars gave a little bit of light, but it was still quite dark and very hard to see. At this time, there were no people, only birds and animals, and among the birds were Dinewan, the emu, and her friend Bralgah, the crane.

One day, Dinewan and Bralgah were quarreling. They quarreled and argued and argued and quarreled until finally Bralgah became so angry that she took one of Dinewan's enormous eggs in her beak and flung it up into the sky. The egg flew up, up, up, but then it hit a pile of firewood, where it split open. The yellow yolk leaked onto the firewood and burst into flame

A great light spilled forth from the fire, light strong and bright enough to light up the whole world. All the birds and animals looked up at the sky and gasped. They had never seen a light so bright. They had never seen so much light at all. Not knowing how foolish it was to stare at such a bright light, some animals nearly blinded themselves by looking at it too long.

A sky spirit saw the blazing fire. He saw how well it lit up everything all over the world. The spirit thought, "I would like to have this fire burn every day. I will kindle it every morning, and it will go out every evening. Then there will be day and night."

When the fire started burning low, the sky spirit did not rekindle it. He let it go out. When it was out, he gathered together his servants, and they went to collect wood. They piled the wood up, and when the time was right, they said to the Morning Star, "Go and shine in the sky! Let everyone know that the great fire will soon be lit!"

The Morning Star went up into the sky and shone brightly. But some creatures were still sleeping, and so they didn't know that day was coming. The sky spirit and his helpers thought that it would be good to also have a sound to help wake sleeping creatures at dawn. They listened to the sounds made by all kinds of animals and birds, but none were loud enough. Then one day, they heard the laugh of a bird called Kookaburra. What a laugh it was! It was very, very loud, and it was deemed to be a good sound to wake up even the deepest sleeper.

The sky spirit went to Kookaburra and said, "I like the sound you make very much. It is very loud and will wake all the sleeping creatures. Please laugh every morning when the Morning Star rises so that all the creatures know it is time to get up."

Kookaburra replied, "I don't want to do that. It seems to be a difficult task, to be the one to get up before dawn every morning and wake up all the other creatures. Please go and ask someone else."

The sky spirit said, "We listened to the sounds of all the other animals. Your sound is the only one that is loud enough. You must do this duty; otherwise my servants and I will never light the great fire again."

"Well, if that is the case," said Kookaburra, "then I will laugh as loudly as I can every morning. I don't want the other creatures to think that it's my fault that there is no great light in the sky anymore."

And so it was that the sky spirit and his servants collected wood every night and kindled a new fire every morning. In the morning, the fire is only starting to burn, so it is neither very bright nor very hot. But as the day goes on, more and more of the wood catches fire, so that in the middle of the day, all of it is burning at once, and it is very hot and very bright. As the day goes on, the firewood is burned up, until at sunset only some glowing coals are left, and when the last coal has gone out, it is nighttime again.

And so it is that parents tell their children never to imitate the call of Kookaburra. "He might think you are making fun of him," say the parents, "and then he might never laugh again, and the whole world will be dark forever."

How the Morning Star Was Made

In several Australian myths, new celestial objects are sometimes created not as a reward for good or heroic behavior but rather as a consequence of perfidy. In this story, the cannibal Mullyan and his wives are punished for their crimes by being burned to death, but Mullyan manages to escape into the heavens where he, his wife, and his disembodied arm become stars.

In the Dreamtime, when animals still walked and looked like people, there was an eagle hawk named Mullyan. He lived in a hut at the end of a branch at the very top of a tall yaraan tree with his wife, Moodai the opossum, and Moodai's mother, who also was named Moodai. Moodai's friend Buttergah lived with them as well. Buttergah was a flying squirrel.

Now, one very important and very frightening thing about this family was that they were all cannibals. Every day, Mullyan would go out with his special hunting spear. He'd find people who were out in the bush on their own, who were too far from their families and friends to call for help, kill them, and then bring them home for his wife to cook for supper. Once the person was cooked nicely, Mullyan, his wife, his mother-in-law, and his wife's friend would all sit down and feast.

Mullyan continued this way of hunting for a long time, but eventually the friends and families of the people that Mullyan and the others had eaten began to wonder why so many people had disappeared without a trace.

"We can't let this continue," said one man, whose camp had lost five people in the past two weeks. "We need to stop whatever it is that keeps taking people away."

"Yes," said another, "but how will we do that?"

A third man said, "Well, all we really need to do is wait until whatever it is takes someone else and then see whether we can track it down from there."

The people all felt sick at heart at this grim suggestion, because it meant that at least one more person would have to disappear before they could solve the problem, but no one else had any better ideas.

It didn't take long before one of the hunters from the camp went missing. His friends took up their weapons and followed his tracks until they found the place where Mullyan had killed him. Then they followed Mullyan's tracks all the way back to the foot of his yaraan tree. They could see the hut high up in the branches, but no one was able to climb the straight, smooth trunk of the tree.

"This is useless," said one man, after he and several others had tried to climb the tree. "We'll never get to them that way."

"We might not, but I know people who can," said another. "The Bibbees are woodpeckers, and they are famous climbers. I think we should also ask Murrowandah the Climbing Rat. They are all friendly to us, and I think they will help us if we ask."

The men of the camp chose their swiftest runners to go and fetch help from among the woodpeckers and climbing rats. Two young Bibbees came back to the camp, as did Murrowandah. "Tell us what you need us to do, and we'll get it done!" they said.

The people explained that Mullyan and his family had been hunting and eating people from their camp but that they lived at the top of a very tall yaraan tree that no one could climb.

"We know that you are all expert climbers," said the camp elder to the Bibbees and Murrowandah. "We need you to climb up to Mullyan's hut and deal with him and his family."

"I know just what we should do," said Murrowandah. "We'll start in the morning."

At sunrise, the Bibbees and Murrowandah began climbing up the tree. They went as stealthily as they could, keeping a sharp eye out for Mullyan and his family. When Mullyan left the hut to go hunting, the Bibbees and Murrowandah hid themselves on the opposite side of the trunk from where he was until he was gone. Then they continued their climb until they reached the hut.

Silently, they stole into the hut without any of the women seeing or hearing them. They poached a burning stick from the fireplace, then hid it in one corner of the hut, where it began to smolder. Then the Bibbees and Murrowandah went back down the tree as quickly and as quietly as they could.

"So, are they all dead?" asked the people when the birds and the rat were back on the ground.

"Not yet," said the rat. "We hid a burning stick inside the wall of their hut. It will take a while for the hut to catch fire. But meanwhile I think everyone here should move away because if the whole tree goes up, it might fall down on someone, and that would be a bad thing."

The people agreed with this plan. They moved to a safe distance and watched and waited to see what would become of Mullyan and his women.

In the hut at the top of the tree, Moodai, Mullyan's wife, sniffed the air. "Do you smell that?" she said.

"Smell what?" said her mother.

"Smoke," said Moodai.

"Well, of course I smell smoke, silly," said her mother. "We just made up the fire so that we can cook whoever your husband brings back for supper."

Moodai wasn't sure her mother was right, but she didn't want to cause a fuss.

A little while later, she heard a crackling sound.

"Did you hear that?" she said.

"Hear what?" said her mother.

"That crackling sound. It was like sticks crackling in a fire," said Moodai.

"Well, of course there are sticks crackling in the fire, silly," said her mother. "That's what happens when you light a fire made of sticks like we did."

Again, Moodai thought that maybe her mother was wrong, but she didn't feel like getting into an argument with the old woman right before her husband was supposed to be getting home.

It was late afternoon when Mullyan came home. He had been out hunting all day and hadn't found anyone to kill and eat for supper. He was tired and grouchy, and when he saw that the hut was full of smoke, he became very angry.

"Put out that fire, will you?" he said. "It's not like I brought anything back to cook, and I can barely breathe in here. Put the fire out so that I can get some rest."

Mullyan went to his sleeping place and lay down while the women put out the fire. But the smoke didn't clear. Mullyan sat up and said, "I thought I told you to put out the fire!"

"We did!" said Buttergah. "See? It's completely out."

"Then why is this place still full of smoke?" said Mullyan.

No sooner had he said that than the spot where the rat had hidden the burning stick roared into flame. Mullyan and his family tried desperately to put out the fire, but their efforts were all in vain. Mullyan's arm was burned off, and the feet of his wife and his mother-in-law were singed black, as was the fur of Buttergah. But this was not the end of their woes. They were unable to escape the flames, and so they burned right up along with their hut until nothing but ashes and bones were left.

Now, the people on the ground had spent the whole day watching the growing billows of smoke, and when flames burst out from the end of the hut, they cheered. The cheer grew to a joyful roar when the whole hut was enveloped in flames. Everyone was so happy and relieved, as well as incredibly grateful to the Bibbees and Murrowandah for their help. Finally all the people would be safe from those horrible cannibals.

And yes, they were indeed safe, but this wasn't the end of Mullyan, no indeed. He rose into the sky, where he became Mullyangah, the Morning Star. He took with him his burned-off arm, which became a small star, and his wife, Moodai, who became a larger star. And there they are in the sky to this day.

The Tale of the Maimai

The seven stars of the Pleiades are the subject of myths from around the world, and Australia is no exception. In this story, the Pleiades are created when two sisters who have been kidnapped by the culture hero Wurrunna join the other five sisters who have already gone to live in the sky.

Once there was a man named Wurrunna, who quarreled with his people. Wurrunna became so angry that he decided to leave his home and travel around the world looking for a better place to live. He had many adventures on his way. One time, he came across a tribe of people who had no eyes. "How do you see?" asked Wurrunna. "We see through our noses," said the people. Another time, Wurrunna slept near a lake of good, fresh water, but when he awoke in the morning, the lake was gone as though it had never been there. Wurrunna had all these adventures and more as he wandered through the world looking for a better place to live.

Finally Wurrunna arrived at a camp where there were seven young women. Wurrunna went into the camp and said, "Please, may I stay here with you for tonight? I have been wandering through the world for a long time, and I am tired and hungry and thirsty."

The young women welcomed Wurrunna gladly. They gave him food and drink and invited him to stay in their camp for the night. When Wurrunna asked who they were, the young women said, "We are called the Maimai. We are wandering, too. We like to go to new places and meet new people."

Wurrunna had never seen such beautiful young women. He decided that one of them should be his wife. That night, he went to sleep without saying anything about his desire to the women, and in the morning, he thanked them and walked away from their camp as though he were continuing his journey. When he thought he had gone far enough that the women could no longer see him, Wurrunna hid himself and waited to see what the women would do. "Maybe I can catch one of them," he thought, "and then I will have a beautiful wife. I am tired of being alone all the time."

Soon enough, Wurrunna saw the young women leave their camp, carrying their digging sticks. They went over to a nest of flying ants. The women poked at the nest with their sticks, and when enough of the nest had been unearthed, the women put down their sticks and began to eat the grubs.

While the women weren't looking, Wurrunna stealthily left his hiding place, stole two of the sticks, then went back to hide again. The women finished their meal and went to pick up their sticks. "Where are our sticks?" said two of the girls. "We laid them right there."

"We don't know," said the others. "We are going back to our camp. You can stay here and look for your sticks."

The two young women looked everywhere for their sticks. When they came close enough to Wurrunna's hiding place, he jumped out and grabbed them. The women struggled to get away, but they could not break Wurrunna's hold. They screamed for their sisters to come and help them, but their sisters were already too far away to hear them. Finally, Wurrunna said, "Stop struggling, or I will hurt you. Stop struggling, and let me tell you what I want. I want you to be my wives. I promise I will treat you very well, if you stop fighting me."

The women reluctantly agreed to be wives to Wurrunna. Together, the three of them traveled onward. "You do understand that our family will notice we are missing," said the girls. "They will come looking for us, and they will not be gentle when they find you."

After hearing this, Wurrunna decided that they must travel on farther yet. He traveled with the women for some days and noticed that they seemed to be settling into a peaceful life with him. But whenever Wurrunna went out hunting, the women spoke to each other about how they might get back to their family and whether their family was even still looking for them.

One day, they stopped and made camp. Not far away was a stand of pine trees. "Go and cut some pine bark for our campfire," said Wurrunna.

"Oh, no," said the women. "We mustn't do that."

"Do as I say," said Wurrunna. "I am your husband, and I tell you to go cut pine bark."

The women answered, "If we cut the pine bark, you will never see us again."

"Stop your foolishness," said Wurrunna. "Take your hatchets, and get some pine bark for our fire. Get it now."

The women took their hatchets and walked over to the pine trees, while Wurrunna remained in the camp. Each woman chose a tree and swung her hatchet at the trunk. As soon as the hatchets bit into the wood, the trees began to grow. Hanging onto their hatchets, the women were pulled up away from the ground as the trees grew taller and taller.

Back at the camp, Wurrunna wondered why he was not hearing any more sounds of wood being chopped. He went over to the stand of pine trees and saw his wives being borne higher and higher into the sky by their trees.

The two women looked up into the sky, and there they saw their five sisters. "Climb up the branches of your trees," said the five sisters.

"Climb up as high as you can, then give us your hands. You must come and live with us in the sky."

The two women did as their sisters bid them. They climbed up, up, up to the very tops of their trees, where they gave their hands to their sisters in the sky. The five sisters helped the two get up into the sky with them, and there the seven of them shine together to this very day.

Kandju's Boomerang

Uluru is a massive sandstone formation that stands above the plains of central Australia, in the southern part of the Northern Territory. Uluru, which was called Ayers Rock by white colonists, is sacred to the Pitjantjatjara Anangu people, who are indigenous to the area around Uluru. Ownership of Uluru was returned to the Pitjantjatjara in 1985, but a ban on climbing the monolith (something Indigenous Australians view as sacrilegious) was not put in place until late 2019.

The sides of Uluru are scored with many grooves and dotted with holes and caves. These features naturally became the subject of myths surrounding the creation and history of Uluru. One such is the legend of Kandju and his boomerang. Like many of the characters in Dreamtime myths, Kandju is both lizard and man simultaneously. In this myth, Kandju creates the scorings on Uluru's face when he tries to dig his boomerang out of the sandstone. The tale retold here is only one of many myths surrounding Kandju's activities, which created many other features on and around Uluru and which are a part of the sacred nature of that place.

In the Dreamtime, there was a lizard-man named Kandju. Kandju was the best boomerang thrower in the whole world. No one could throw a boomerang as far as Kandju could, and no one could throw it more accurately. Kandju also was very good at making boomerangs. He made many fine boomerangs for himself and used them when he went hunting. Sometimes he threw them just for the pleasure of it and to see just how far he could make them go.

One day, Kandju went out into the bush with his best boomerang. He wanted to see how far he could throw it. After a few practice throws, he hurled the boomerang with all his might and skill. The boomerang flew through the air, going farther and farther and farther until it buried itself deep into the sandstone of Uluru, the great rock that rises high above the flat bush in the middle of Australia.

Kandju waited a very long time for his boomerang to come back. He waited and waited and waited, and finally he said to himself, "Even I can't throw a boomerang that far. Something must have happened to it." So Kandju set out in the direction he had thrown the boomerang, looking all the while to see where it had landed or what it had struck.

After a very long journey, he finally arrived at Uluru. There he found his boomerang, stuck deep into the sandstone.

"Oh, no!" said Kandju. "That is my very best boomerang! I have to get it back!"

Kandju began to scrabble at the rock, trying and trying to free his boomerang. After much digging, he finally got the boomerang back, which made him very happy. But the traces of his digging are still there on the face of Uluru to this very day, in the deep scorings of the rock that run down its surface.

Part II: Gods, Heroes, and Monsters

The Wives of Baiame

Baiame is the creator-god of several tribes in southern Australia. Besides having made the world, Baiame also functions as a hero who braves various dangers and comes out victorious.

In this tale, Baiame must rescue his wives from the crocodiles that have swallowed them, and in the process, he creates Narran Lake in north-central New South Wales. To effect the rescue, Baiame uses two traditional Indigenous Australian weapons, the woomera *and the* nulla-nulla. *A* woomera *is a throwing stick, something like an atlatl, and is used to give greater power and distance to a spear throw. A* nulla-nulla *is a club used for hunting. The* dilly bags *used by the women are traditionally woven from plant fibers.*

Baiame it was who made the world, and when his work of creation was done, he lived in the world for a time with his wives, who were named Birra-nulu and Kunnan-beili. One day, Baiame said to his wives, "I am going to go out looking for honey. Take your digging sticks and go find some yams and frogs. We will meet at Coorigil Spring. It's a good place to make camp. But be careful! The water in the spring is only for drinking, not for bathing. Stay out of the water!"

And so Baiame went out to find honey, while his wives set out for the place where the yams were growing. They dug many yams, then went to a pond where there were many frogs. When they had caught enough frogs, they went to the spring and made a shelter for them to sleep in with their husband, as well as a place to store their food.

When the wives' work was done, Baiame had not yet returned from his task. The day was very hot, and both women had been working very hard, and the water of the spring was cool and clear.

"Let's go for a swim," said Birra-nulu. "It's so hot, and the water looks so inviting."

"No, we mustn't!" said Kunnan-beili. "Baiame told us not to."

The women argued over this for a little while, but in the end Kunnan-beili gave in. They both took off their clothing and jumped into the water. The water was clear and cool and lovely to feel on their skin. The women paddled about in it happily for a little while, until suddenly two great Kurreahs, the crocodiles who guarded the spring, swam up from the depths and swallowed the women whole.

Now, the Kurreahs well knew that they had just eaten the wives of Baiame, and they knew they had to get away quickly if they were to escape his anger. The Kurreahs swam down, down, down deep under the waters of the pool, where there was a channel that brought water to the spring from the Narran River. The Kurreahs squeezed themselves into the channel, blocking the flow of water. As they pushed their bodies through the channel, they also pushed the water in front of them. They moved so fast that they created a huge wave of water that surged out the end of the channel and out the other end. The wave was so large, it made the river overspill its banks, and when the wave had finally passed, the bed of the river was completely dry.

The Kurreahs began to hurry down the course of the riverbed, knowing that Baiame likely would come looking for them very soon indeed. And the Kurreahs were correct: while they had been scrambling through the channel and pushing all the water out of the river, Baiame returned to the camp with a good quantity of honey. He put down the honey and called to his wives. They did not answer. The only sounds were the calls of birds and the croaking of the frogs that the women had collected in their dilly bags. Baiame looked about and noticed that the level of the spring was much, much lower than it had been when he left. He looked some more, and found his wives' clothing at the side of the spring. Then he looked more closely at the spring, and he noticed the mouth of the channel that the Kurreahs had used for their escape.

"Aha!" thought Baiame. "My wives disobeyed me, and the Kurreahs swallowed them up!"

Grasping his weapons in his hands, Baiame went into the channel and began to crawl along it. Soon enough, he came out the other side and saw that the riverbed had dried up. He climbed up onto the bank of the now-dry river and looked along the length of the riverbed. As he scrambled up the bank, he dislodged pebbles and rocks, and these became the ridges that run along the Narran River today.

When Baiame got to the top of the riverbank, he spied the two Kurreahs in the distance, hurrying along as fast as their slow bodies could take them on dry land. Baiame sped along the riverbank, and soon he arrived at a place where the water spread out to make a shallow lake. He knew that the Kurreahs would be making for this lake, so he readied his weapons and waited for the great crocodiles to arrive.

It did not take long before the surge of water that the Kurreahs were pushing along in front of them came into the lake, with the Kurreahs close behind it. As soon as the Kurreahs climbed up onto the shore,

Baiame took his woomera and fitted his spear into it. He threw the spear with all his might, and it flew at the first Kurreah, impaling it through the head. Then he ran over to the second Kurreah and struck it with his nulla-nulla. While it was stunned, Baiame took his knife and slit its throat. Then he did the same to the first Kurreah.

The bodies of the Kurreahs thrashed heavily to and fro in their death agony. When the Kurreahs were both quite dead, Baiame took his knife and slit their bellies open. The women's bodies tumbled out onto the riverbank, unmoving and all covered in slime. Baiame looked about and saw a large nest of red ants. He gathered up a large number of ants and put them onto his wives' bodies. The ants scurried across the women's bodies, licking up the slime and occasionally stinging and nipping at the women's skin. After a time, the tickling of the ants' feet and their stings and bites began to rouse the women.

The women opened their eyes and saw Baiame looking down at them. Shamefacedly, they stood before him.

"We are sorry we disobeyed you," they said. "You told us how we could keep ourselves safe, and we didn't listen."

"Yes, and you were fortunate that I came back to the camp when I did. If you had been in the bellies of the Kurreahs much longer, there wouldn't have been enough of you left for me to revive. Maybe next time you will listen to me?"

"Oh, yes!" said the women. "We will never go swimming without your permission ever again!"

Then Baiame looked at the grooves and depressions in the earth that had been made by the thrashings of the Kurreahs.

"Let these fill with water, and let the waters join together and make a lake," he said, "and let many water birds gather here."

And that is how Narran Lake was made.

Bahloo and His Dogs

Bahloo is simultaneously the moon itself and the god of the moon. Like many gods, he has the power to grant or deny eternal life. In this just-so story, we learn why humans must remain mortal. They have to make a dreadful choice whether to handle deadly snakes, which might bite and kill them but will grant them eternal life, or decline to hold the snakes, a decision that will keep them mortal.

Although the theme of this story is quite serious, it does have a certain comic element. The humor resides in Bahloo's insistence that the deadly snakes he owns as pets are actually his "dogs" that he takes out for walks, as though his slithery friends were really canines instead.

One thing that Bahloo, the Moon, liked to do very much was to take his dogs for a walk. He had three dogs, and he was very pleased with them. Except they weren't really dogs. Bahloo's "dogs" were actually snakes of the deadliest kind. Bahloo had three of them: a death adder, a tiger snake, and a black snake.

Sometimes Bahloo walked about with his dogs at night. Sometimes he walked about with them in the daytime. During one of those daytime rambles, Bahloo came across some men who were hunting and fishing along a river.

"Greetings, Bahloo!" called the men. "Come and sit a while in our camp!"

"Greetings!" called Bahloo. "I would love to sit with you, but I am walking my dogs just now and I mustn't stop. We want to go to the other side of the river, but I can't get myself and my dogs across at the same time. Would you please take my dogs across for me?"

The men hesitated. They didn't want to offend Bahloo, but they also wanted to stay alive. "Oh, no, Bahloo," said the men. "Please forgive us, but we can't take your dogs across."

"Whyever not?" said Bahloo. He picked up his dogs, and they wrapped themselves comfortably around his neck and arms. "See? They're really quite tame."

"They are tame for you, Bahloo, but not for us," said the men. "Your dogs are good dogs, we're sure, but they have venom in their fangs, and they would bite if anyone but you tried to touch them. If they bite us, we will die. We cannot carry your dogs across the river."

"Let me show you something," said Bahloo. He picked up a piece of bark in one hand and a stone in the other. "Look at the bark. I'm going to throw it in the river. Watch what it does."

Bahloo threw the bark into the river. It floated gently on the surface and was carried downstream by the current. "If you carry my dogs for me, you will be like that piece of bark. You will not die, but you will come back to life and live again. Now watch this stone," he said, as he threw the stone into the river, where it promptly sank. "If you refuse to carry my dogs, you will be like the stone. You will die, and you will never come back again."

"Bahloo, your gift of eternal life is generous, but it is one we cannot accept," said the men. "We cannot carry your dogs for you. We are too frightened of them and do not want to be bitten. Please forgive us."

"Very well," said Bahloo. "You had your chance. You refused to help me. From now on, when people die, they will stay dead forever. Now come along," he said to his dogs. "We need to get across the river."

Bahloo waded into the river. The men watched him cross to the other side, where he continued his journey without ever once looking back. From that day forward, Bahloo never came down to walk his dogs or talk to the people ever again, but he sent many more snakes to live on the earth, where they gave much trouble to the people. And so it is that when people die, they stay dead forever, and so it is that when the people see one of Bahloo's "dogs," they kill it as soon as possible.

The Winjarning Brothers and Cheeroonear

The Winjarning Brothers are semi-divine heroes who travel to various places in order to help those in need. In this story, they rescue a camp of people from the monstrous Cheeroonear and his equally monstrous wife and hunting dogs. In this tale, the heroes fight and defeat the monsters not only with strength of arms but with cunning and the help of the people they are trying to save.

This tale revolves in part around the problem of access to water. Much of Australia is arid, and in some parts of the country, water lies under the surface rather than pooling in billabongs *(oxbow lakes that form when a river changes course) or running in rivers. This water may be accessed by turning over rocks that conceal the springs that flow beneath them, an action that we see Cheeroonear perform in this legend.*

Once there was a fearsome creature named Cheeroonear, who lived and hunted with his dogs on the Nullarbor Plain. Cheeroonear was enormously tall and had the head of a dog with the lower jaw of a pelican. The pelican's pouch reached from his jaw down to the hollow in the middle of his body, just where the ribs should come together. Except the ribs didn't come together on Cheeroonear's body; instead, he had two separate sides, one of which contained his lungs and the other of which contained his heart.

Now, not only was Cheeroonear a giant, but he also had gigantically long arms that went all the way from his shoulders to his ankles. But perhaps the most frightening thing about this creature was his taste for human flesh. He thought that the best dinner in the world was the meat he got from the unfortunate human beings he stole from their camps or caught out in the bush.

No one had ever seen Cheeroonear, although hunters sometimes came across his tracks. And everyone knew what had happened when someone from their band disappeared, because soon enough someone would go out to hunt or look for yams or honey and come across a pile of human bones with the marks of teeth on them.

There came a time when there had been no rain, and one day after another was as hot as it could be. Waterholes and streams dried up, and there was no respite from the heat. People, animals, and birds found shade and shelter wherever they could, but nothing they could find gave them relief.

One day, in the midst of this unbearable heat, some people were sitting in the shade of trees at the top of a hill near one of the last watering holes. They were too tired and too thirsty and too scorched to do much of anything except sit there and look out over the plain and wait for the heat to go away and the rain to come again. One man looked out over the plain and saw something or someone in the distance. It was walking toward the watering hole. As it got closer, the man's blood ran cold, despite the oppressive heat. The creature wasn't a human being at all. It was Cheeroonear, and he was walking straight toward the place where the people were.

The man turned to his family and friends and said, "Get up! Move! Hide yourselves! Cheeroonear is coming!"

The people groaned and told the man to sit down and be quiet, but he persisted. "Look! Right there! He's headed straight for us, and he'll eat us all for sure if we don't hide!"

The people looked in the direction the man was pointing, and there, sure enough, was the eight-foot-tall, dog-headed Cheeroonear striding toward them, with his knuckles dragging in the dust. As fast as they could manage in their parched state, the people scrambled to hide behind trees and rocks. They sat as still as they could and hoped that Cheeroonear would pass them by without noticing they were there.

Cheeroonear came closer and closer. When he got to the waterhole, he took off the rock that covered the water, then knelt and drank. He drank and drank and drank, and the people could see Cheeroonear's great pouch filling with water. When he had had enough to drink, Cheeroonear stood up. The pouch in the middle of his body was all distended with water. He hadn't taken two steps when he turned and vomited up everything he had drunk. Some human bones came out with the water. When he had finished vomiting, Cheeroonear sniffed the air and looked about.

"I may not be able to see you," said the creature, "but I can smell you, people. I will come back, and I and my wife and my dogs will feast first upon your children and then upon your own corpses."

With that, Cheeroonear turned and walked away from the watering hole. The people sat in their hiding places and shivered, not wanting to move until they were sure the monster was gone. When his thudding footsteps had finally faded away into the distance, the people came out of hiding.

"Oh, whatever shall we do?" said one woman. "How can we protect ourselves against that creature?"

"We will have to lie in wait for it and kill it when it comes back," said a man.

"Yes!" said some other men. "We are many, and he is only one creature. We should kill it."

Then a wise elder spoke. "Yes, you might kill Cheeroonear, but what about his dogs? And maybe we won't have the strength to kill such a beast. Who knows what powers it might have?"

The first man who had spoken said, "We don't have much choice but to try. But you are wise amongst us, and perhaps you know a better plan."

"Oh, yes," said the elder. "I know just what we should do. We should send two of our swiftest runners to go and find the Winjarning Brothers. They are the greatest warriors in the world, and only they will be able to stop Cheeroonear. I saw the younger brother near here on the coast recently. He may still be there. If you can find him, he'll take you to his elder brother, and then you can bring them both back here to help us."

And so the runners headed down toward the coast to see whether they could find the brothers. As it happened, both brothers were together, spending the day at the seaside. The runners saw the two men sitting in the sand. The runners went up to the seated men and said, "Are you the Winjarning Brothers? We have been sent by our camp to find you. We desperately need your help."

The brothers stood up and said, "Yes, we are the Winjarning Brothers. What do you need from us?"

The first runner said, "Our people were taking shelter from the heat under some trees on a hillside when a strange creature came walking toward our watering hole. When it got close enough, we saw that it was Cheeroonear. He drank some water, then vomited it back up. Then he said that he could smell us and said that he would be coming back with his wife and dogs to eat us and all our children! We don't know what to do against such a fearsome monster. Please, come back with us to our camp and help us!"

The brothers said, "We will most certainly help you. We will come to your camp tonight when the moon is high. Prophecy says that once Cheeroonear has been seen by human eyes, his death will be upon him. Tell your people that we are on our way."

The runners returned to their camp with the message that the Winjarning Brothers were coming to help them. Everyone was much gladdened by this, and they waited expectantly for night to fall and for the moon to rise. That night was a full moon, so the whole land was covered in silvery light.

As promised, the Winjarning Brothers arrived just when the moon was at its height. They went into the camp, where they were seen and recognized by the wise elder. "Welcome to our camp," said the elder. "We need your help so very badly. Cheeroonear was here today. He is going to come back with his wife and dogs and eat us and all our children if we don't stop him. You are the best warriors in the whole world. We will do whatever you tell us needs to be done."

"We are pleased to help you," said the eldest brother, "and what we need you to do is this: send all your strongest men into the bush. Have them cut as much brushwood as they can carry and then bring it back here. When we have enough brushwood, we will show you what to do with it."

The men went out into the bush and cut a great quantity of brushwood. When they brought it back, the brothers had them build a channel with it. The channel had two sides, wider at the end that was opposite the camp and so narrow at the top that only one man or one dog might be able to pass through it at a time. Just as they finished the channel, dawn began to break in the east.

The brothers took aside six of the bravest men of the camp and gave them special instructions, and when that was done, the eldest brother said to the men of the camp, "Go and get your weapons and stand at the ready along the walls of the channel. It will be your job to stop any of the dogs if they get through the walls. But if the dogs come up the channel and go through the opening here, we will take care of them. The women and children should go and hide themselves as best they can. You six men know what to do. Be on your guard."

Soon everyone was in position, and the only thing to be done was to wait. They didn't have to wait long. The morning breeze carried the sound of baying dogs into the camp. It was an unearthly sound, and everyone who heard it knew that they were hearing the bays of Cheeroonear's hunting pack. The baying didn't last long; the dogs finished their run up toward the camp in total silence.

When the dogs got close enough that the people could see them, the people quailed. These were monstrous dogs, as high at the shoulder as a grown man is tall, with mouths full of teeth as sharp as the sharpest flint. The dogs entered the bottom of the channel, running in a line. When the first dog reached the top of the channel, the youngest brother clubbed it on the head with his boomerang, killing it quickly. Then the brother cut off its tail and handed it to one of the six picked men. The next dog came to the top of the channel, and the eldest brother dispatched it with one thrust of his spear. The elder brother cut off that dog's tail and handed it to another of the picked men. In this way, the brothers killed all six of Cheeroonear's dogs, one by one, and gave the tails to the picked men.

Once all the dogs had been killed, everyone knew that Cheeroonear would be on his way. The Winjarning Brothers put into action the next part of their plan. They prayed fervently to the god who controls the mists, that he might send a fog down upon their camp and obscure everything from Cheeroonear's sight. In answer to their prayer, a thick fog came down, blanketing everything in mist. From their hiding places, the women and children wailed as though they were terrified, while the six bravest men took the severed tails of the monstrous dogs and waved them as though the dogs were still alive and happily killing all the people in the camp.

Not long after the fog came down, the people heard the footsteps of Cheeroonear coming up the channel that the men had built. They heard his ragged breathing. Everyone was very frightened, but they continued playing the parts the brothers had assigned them.

When Cheeroonear came near the top of the channel, he heard the cries of the women and children, and saw the dogs' tails wagging in the mist. "Good, good!" he chuckled to himself. "My dogs are making short work of these people. My wife and dogs and I will all feast well tonight!"

Thinking that the people were already as good as dead, Cheeroonear was not on his guard as he came to the top of the channel. He took one last step toward the opening between the piles of brush, and then the Winjarning Brothers were upon him, striking blow after blow after blow with their nulla-nullas. Soon Cheeroonear's battered body lay dead at the top of the channel.

The men of the camp began to cheer, and the women and children began to come out of their hiding places, but the Winjarning Brothers said, "No, wait! Stay where you are, and stay vigilant, for there may be danger yet!"

Back at Cheeroonear's camp, Cheeroonear's monstrous wife wondered what was taking her husband and his dogs so long. She set out toward the camp, and when she approached the channel the men had made, she heard the sound of dogs barking. She thought this was the sound of her husband's pack, but in fact it was the six picked men, who were all waving the severed dogs' tails and barking to make Cheeroonear's wife think that nothing was amiss.

When Cheeroonear's wife got to the body of her husband, she stopped to look at it. In a flash, the Winjarning Brothers darted through the channel gate and killed her with their clubs. They were joined by the men and women of the camp, who struck her with boomerangs, with sticks, and with rocks. When they were sure the monstrous woman was dead, some of the men took their hatchets and cut the body in two. From one of the halves emerged a creature that looked like a twelve-year-old boy.

At first, the men were too surprised to do or say anything, but then the younger Winjarning Brother said, "Catch him!" The men of the tribe jumped toward the boy, trying to obey the command, but the boy turned himself into a serpent that slithered quickly away before the men were able to grab him. The boy in fact was an evil, shapeshifting spirit, who still plagues the bush even today. Sometimes he has the form of a man, sometimes a bird, and at other times he is a reptile.

And of Cheeroonear and his wife and dogs there was no further sign, except for some footprints that are still visible in the earth.

Wyju the Traveler

Sometimes heroes help other people, and sometimes they themselves require saving. Although this story primarily is about the hero Wyju, the Winjarning Brothers also make an appearance as Wyju's rescuers when he falls afoul of the jealous Kirkin. In addition to showing Wyju's cunning and strength, this tale also explains the presence of red ochre in the soil. Ochre of all kinds is used for various purposes by Indigenous Australians. Some of these purposes are sacred, such as body decoration for ceremonies, while others, such as a form of sunscreen, are more mundane.

Wyju's defeat of the Great Serpent involves the use of mallee root. Mallee shrubs are a kind of eucalypt species native to Australia. They have a long, thick root called a lignotuber that often is full of water.

Wyju was a man who enjoyed a solitary life. He traveled from camp to camp, and wherever he went, he helped those who were in need. One day, he came to a place where the people were mourning and weeping. "What has happened?" Wyju asked.

"Oh, this is a sad day!" said one man. "The Great Snake came into our camp and swallowed our child whole!"

"Why do you not pursue the snake and kill it?" said Wyju.

"Because it is no ordinary serpent. If we kill it, the water will cease to flow, and we will all die of thirst."

"Even magical serpents can be killed," said Wyju. "Do you know how it might be done?"

"Yes," said the father of the child. "It can be killed when its body is stretched all the way out in a line. Then the water will continue to flow even if it is dead. But if you kill it when it is coiled up or when its body is in any way bent, it will dry up all the springs in revenge."

"Leave it to me," said Wyju. "I will get your child back and secure your water supply at the same time."

One of the people of the camp led Wyju to the place where the snake was coiled up under a tree, asleep. "I dare not stay," said the man. "It must not see me, or it will think my people are up to something, and I do not want to risk its wrath."

Once the man had crept quietly away, Wyju watched the snake and thought about how he might go about killing it. Nearby there was a stand of mallee shrubs. Wyju took the long root of one of the mallees and climbed up the tree under which the snake was sleeping. He went out on the branch that spread over the snake, trimmed off the end of the mallee root, and held it out above the snake's head. Water started to drip out of the mallee root. Drop after drop landed on the snake's head, right between its eyes.

Soon the snake was awakened by the dripping water. It fluttered its tongue and tasted some of the water that dripped down its snout. The snake raised its head, looking for the source of the water. It began to extend its body upward, following the trail of drops. Up, up, up the snake's body went, until it was stretched out in a straight line with nothing but the tip of its tail touching the ground.

Wyju seized the moment. He grabbed the snake around its neck and plunged his knife into it, then slid down its body, slicing it open with the knife as he descended. When the knife slit the snake's belly open, the child tumbled out, badly frightened but otherwise unharmed. The Great Snake's body fell to the ground, lifeless.

Wyju carried the little one back to her grateful family and told the camp what had happened. The people were very happy that the child had been returned alive and even happier that the serpent no longer controlled their water supply. They made a great feast to honor Wyju and to celebrate the child's good fortune.

In the middle of the feast, one of the men of the camp said to Wyju, "I have a niece who is of an age to be wed. Our family would be honored if you would consent to be her husband."

"I am honored to be asked," Wyju replied, "but I will never marry. I live a solitary life, traveling about. I would never be home for very long, and that's no life for a good woman, to have her husband be gone almost all the time."

Wyju stayed in that camp for a few days, and during that time a steady stream of men came to visit him. They all asked whether Wyju would marry their nieces, but every time Wyju gave the same answer. "I will never marry. I live a solitary life, traveling about. I would never be home for very long, and that's no life for a good woman, to have her husband be gone almost all the time." When

Wyju refused the men, they would accept the refusal graciously and then say, "Oh, well. I suppose there's always Kirkin. Maybe if I asked him. I really should go visit him."

Wyju had never heard of Kirkin. He found it odd that one man after another would mention Kirkin and then propose to pay him a visit. Wyju gradually learned who Kirkin was as he spent more time in the camp. Kirkin, it seemed, was an unusually handsome man who had long, golden hair. When Kirkin combed his hair in the sun, it scattered golden rays everywhere, making him look as though he had a halo of light around him. All the men for miles around admired Kirkin greatly and would find excuses to go and visit him. They also encouraged their nieces to marry Kirkin, but the young women one and all refused because Kirkin was vain and could only talk about himself. Also the women were jealous that Kirkin's hair was far more beautiful and lustrous than their own.

Now, at that time, Kirkin wanted a wife for himself but had had no success. Soon word came to Kirkin that every man for miles around had been going to the camp where Wyju was staying to offer their nieces in marriage to the traveler. "Too bad none of the women will have you," said Kirkin's friends when they told him what was happening. "Too bad they only seem to want this Wyju fellow, even though he turns them down every time."

Hearing this made Kirkin very jealous, because he could not understand how anyone could prefer another man to him. He asked where he might find Wyju and then set out to meet him. Soon enough, Kirkin arrived in the camp where Wyju was staying. One of the people of the camp introduced Kirkin to Wyju. Kirkin said, "You have been here for some time, yet you have not come to visit me. Do you not see my golden hair? Men have made pilgrimages from very far away indeed just to see it."

"Yes, I do see your hair," said Wyju, "but I did not think I needed to meet you, since all the men here already told me so many good things about you."

Kirkin was unsure whether what Wyju said was a compliment. In his jealousy, he decided it was not, and he hit upon a plan to get rid of Wyju once and for all.

"Would you like to come hunting with me tomorrow?" said Kirkin. "There's a creature around here called a walliow. It looks something like a kangaroo rat, but larger. When it's roasted, it has the best flavor of any meat you've ever tasted. What do you say? Shall we hunt together tomorrow?"

"Yes," said Wyju. "I will be pleased to come with you. I will be ready early in the morning."

Kirkin said goodbye and left the camp. But instead of going home, he went out into the bush where a great deal of long grass was growing. He took his digging stick and dug a deep hole. He planted many sharp spikes at the bottom. Then he covered the trap with sticks, on top of which he placed turves that had long grass sticking out of them, so that no one could tell that there was anything strange there at all. Then Kirkin killed a small animal, tied a bit of string to it, and placed it on top of the trap. When everything was ready, Kirkin went home, thinking that he would put Wyju firmly in his place.

In the morning, Kirkin met Wyju at the camp where he was staying. Wyju was there waiting for him, his spear in one hand and his boomerang in the other.

"You can bring the spear with you, but you won't need it," said Kirkin. "You won't need the boomerang, either. You can't hunt walliows with those. You have to catch them by jumping on them when they come out of their burrows."

"Very well," said Wyju. "Show me where the walliows are."

Kirkin and Wyju walked into the bush together. Kirkin led Wyju to the place where the long grass grew. "This is where the walliows live," he said. "Walk carefully through the grass. When you see a movement, jump, because it's probably a walliow."

Soon enough, Kirkin led Wyju to the place where the trap was set. "Oh!" cried Kirkin. "I saw something move through the grass! Here, lie down and creep forward. It might be a walliow. But be ready to spring if you see it move."

While Wyju crept through the tall grass toward the trap, Kirkin went to the place where he had laid the other end of the string. As soon as Wyju was close enough, Kirkin pulled on the string, making the dead animal move as though it were alive.

"A walliow!" whispered Wyju. "Did you see it?"

"Yes, I did," said Kirkin. "Wait a bit and see whether it moves again. If it does, jump."

Again Kirkin pulled on the end of the string, making the dead animal move. Wyju gathered himself for a spring, then jumped feet first onto the flimsy covering of the trap. He fell down into the pit Kirkin had made, and his feet and legs were cruelly pierced by the spikes that had been planted in the floor of the pit.

Wyju screamed in pain and fear. "Kirkin! Kirkin! Oh, help me, please! Someone laid a trap with spikes, and my feet and legs are all pierced!"

Kirkin made no move to help. Instead, he looked over the lip of the pit and laughed. "You may be a great traveler, but you certainly are not very wise. Also I somehow doubt that any of the women around here will be interested in you once you've been down there a while. Goodbye, my friend."

As Kirkin strode away, Wyju began to weep. He tried to get free of the spikes but was unable to. His blood flowed so freely that it filled the bottom of the pit and seeped into the earth all around that place, turning it to red ochre, and today men still go to that place to find ochre with which to paint their bodies.

When Wyju was too weary and in too much pain to struggle further, he began to pray. "O Great Spirit, hear my prayer! O Baiame, creator of all the world, listen to me! I am caught in a pit, and I am grievously wounded. Send aid to me, as I have given aid to others in my travels."

Baiame heard Wyju's prayer and saw his cruel plight. Baiame called to the Winjarning Brothers. He told them to go to Wyju and rescue him from the pit and to heal his wounds. "Do not delay," said Baiame. "Rescue Wyju as soon as you can. He is beloved of me because he always tries to help people wherever he goes."

The Winjarning Brothers went to Wyju with all the speed they could muster. They helped the injured man out of the pit, and pulled the cruel spikes out of his legs and feet. They touched all the places Wyju had been hurt, and healed all of his wounds. Then they bade Wyju farewell and returned to Baiame.

After the brothers had gone, Wyju took up his weapons and headed toward the place where Kirkin lived. He found a place to hide himself and waited until dawn, when he knew that Kirkin would stand tall and let the sunlight glitter in his hair for all to see.

Sure enough, when the sun rose in the morning, Kirkin stood forth and began combing his lustrous hair. Wyju stood up from his hiding place and threw his boomerang at Kirkin. The boomerang sliced through Kirkin's neck, and his head and body went tumbling to the ground. Wyju made a pyre out of brushwood and burned Kirkin's body on it. Soon all that remained of the handsome man with the golden hair was a small bird that flew out of his body as the flames consumed it. To this day, that bird can be seen hovering in the air, looking for insects to eat. It often flies near fires in the bush, waiting to catch the small creatures that are trying to escape from the flames.

Wyungare and the Wives of Nepelle

This tale from southeastern Australia centers on the heroes Nepelle and Wyungare. Nepelle is a divine figure in his own right and often works with and for the god Nurunderi. Wyungare, on the other hand, is a semi-divine being given by Nepelle and Nurunderi to a grieving widow to be the child she was denied by the premature death of her husband.

Nepelle and Wyungare begin the story as friends, but they end it as enemies when Wyungare steals Nepelle's wives. Nepelle uses magic fire to punish Wyungare and the two women but is unsuccessful in killing them because Wyungare pulls them into the heavens, where they become stars.

Long ago, there were two hunters named Nepelle and Wyungare. They were both handsome and strong, and they never failed to return home with game. When Nepelle and Wyungare hunted, the people of their camp ate well, and they ate well often.

Nepelle was a married man. He had two wives, who were both very beautiful. Wyungare had not yet married, for he had not yet found a woman who pleased him enough.

One day, Wyungare felt very thirsty, for the day had been very hot indeed. He went down to the lake. He picked a hollow reed and knelt next to the water. He put the reed into the water and began to suck at the straw. The water was lovely and cool, and soon his thirst was quenched.

While Wyungare had been drinking at the lake, the two wives of Nepelle walked by. They noticed Wyungare kneeling there. They saw how beautiful his body was and how handsome his face. Both of them immediately fell in love with him. They did not care that they were already married; they had to have Wyungare for themselves.

When Wyungare stood up from getting his drink, he saw the two wives of Nepelle watching him. As soon as they saw him, they both blushed and turned away, then went about their business. Now, Wyungare had often looked upon the wives of Nepelle himself and thought them very beautiful and very desirable, but he had not yet acted on this because he knew Nepelle would be very angry indeed.

That evening, the wives of Nepelle went out into the bush, saying that they were going to look for yams. They took their digging sticks with them, but they had no intention of digging for yams. What they wanted was to be able to speak to one another alone, without their husband or anyone else overhearing them.

"Did you see Wyungare at the lake today?" said the first wife. "He is so handsome!"

"Yes, I did see him!" said the second. "He is even more handsome than Nepelle. I wish we could be married to Wyungare instead."

"I agree. But how are we going to get him to marry us? If we walk up and ask him, he might tell Nepelle, and Nepelle will be very angry indeed."

The first wife thought for a moment, then she said, "I have an idea. I'll tell you about it while we walk back home. And keep an eye out for yams on the way; we should try not to return empty-handed, or people will ask questions."

The wives of Nepelle did manage to find a few yams on the way home, and they prepared them for their husband to eat that night. When their husband was sound asleep, and the camp had settled for the night, the two wives put their plan into action. They went to Wyungare's hut and ran past it, making it sound like they were emus, not women. Being a good hunter, Wyungare was immediately awakened by the sound. He grabbed his spear and ran out of his hut, thinking to catch the emus before they could run too far. But when he got outside, all he saw were the two wives of Nepelle standing in front of him.

"Where did the emus go?" said Wyungare. "Tell me, quickly, so that I can catch them!"

"The emus are right here," said the first wife, pointing to herself and the second wife. "And we have come to catch you."

The second wife said, "Come into the bush with us. We have desired you for a long time. We want you to be our husband instead of Nepelle. Please say you'll come with us!"

At first, Wyungare wavered, but then he saw just how beautiful Nepelle's wives were, and he consented. He invited them into his hut, and they passed the night together in much delight.

In the morning, Wyungare and his new wives woke very early and went out into the bush to go hunting. A few other people in the camp also were up at that time and saw them leave together. When Nepelle woke and found his wives missing, he asked whether anyone had seen them.

"Yes," said one man. "They went into the bush with Wyungare. I saw the three of them come out of his hut early this morning."

Nepelle became very angry. He went to Wyungare's hut and set fire to it. Before the fire could begin to consume the hut, Nepelle told it, "Wait until Wyungare and my two unfaithful wives come back. When they are asleep, come to life, and burn their hut and them inside it. If they get away before you kill them, follow them wherever they go. Do not stop until all three of them are dead."

That evening, Wyungare and the two women returned to the camp with a wallaby Wyungare had caught and some frogs the women had found in a nearby billabong. They shared their catch with the others in the camp and avoided the eye of Nepelle. Soon the sun had set, so Wyungare and the two women went into his hut and went to sleep.

As Nepelle had commanded, the fire leapt into life as soon as the three were asleep. Soon the heat and smoke and roar of the flames woke Wyungare and the two women, who hurried out of the hut as quickly as they possibly could. They ran across the camp and out into the bush, but to their dismay, the fire followed them. No matter how far or how fast they ran, the fire came right behind them, consuming bushes, grasses, and trees and becoming larger and larger the longer it burned.

Wyungare and his wives changed course and made for the lake. They dove into the water, where they were safe for the moment. But the fire followed them to the lakeshore and was greedily consuming the reeds along its edge, and since it was a magical fire, it was not going out as the reeds were consumed.

"What shall we do?" cried the first wife. "Nepelle will never let us escape. If we try to leave the water, the fire will follow us. If we stay here, we will starve or drown. What shall we do?"

"We will go up to the heavens," said Wyungare. "I will make sure all of us are safe."

Wyungare took his barbed spear, which he had grabbed as he fled his burning hut. He hurled the spear with all his might up toward the heavens, where it stuck fast. Wyungare tugged on the line that was attached to the butt of the spear to make sure it was firmly fixed, then he told his wives to climb up. As the flames roared along the lakeshore, the two women climbed and climbed until they reached the heavens. Once Wyungare saw that his wives were safe, he climbed up himself. And there they live to this day as three beautiful stars.

The Frog Man and the Bunyip

As we saw in the story of the Wawilak Sisters, Indigenous Australians often take various animals as their tribal totem. Here, the totem is the frog, and the story functions partly as an explanation why people of the frog totem do not eat their totemic animal.

The villain of this story is the bunyip, a monster native to Australia that lurks around billabongs, rivers, and lakes to stalk, catch, and devour the unwary. The bunyip's defeat leads not only to salvation for the young woman he captures and for her young man, but also to the creation of the moon, which is made from the bunyip's eye.

One night, a young man of the Frog tribe went down to the billabong to hunt ducks. He covered himself in a disguise of reeds, slipped into the water, and sat down so that the water was up to his neck. There he waited silently for an unsuspecting duck to swim toward him. As soon as one was within reach, the man grabbed it by its feet, pulled it under the water, and then broke its neck with one twist. There were many ducks that night, and soon the man had a good catch to bring home to his wife.

Now, a bunyip had also come down to the billabong, thinking to do some hunting of his own because he knew that a camp of people lay not far away. The bunyip hid himself behind a tree and waited for the young man to walk in his direction. Just as the young man had stood up and made a stride toward the bank of the billabong, the bunyip came out from behind his tree, thinking to grab the man and then eat him for supper. The young man saw the bunyip and shouted in fear and surprise. He ran away just as the bunyip reached out to grab him. Fortunately, the young man was a fast runner. All the bunyip managed to get was a handful of the reeds that the young man had worn as a hunting blind.

As the man scrambled out of the water and up the bank of the billabong, his wife came running up to meet him.

"What happened, husband?" she said. "Why did you shout?"

"There's a bunyip in the billabong!" he replied. "It very nearly grabbed me!"

The wife laughed. "Don't be silly. There aren't any bunyips anywhere near here. Now give me those lovely fat ducks you caught, and let's go home to eat."

While the man and his wife stood there talking, the bunyip crept toward them. Just as the young couple turned to head back to their camp, the bunyip's long arms reached up and grabbed the young woman, then it fled back into the darkness of the billabong so quickly that the young man could hardly see where it had gone. He tried bravely to follow, but the bunyip left no trail. Despondent, he went back to his camp and explained to the other people of his tribe what had happened.

"I'm going to get my wife back," said the young man. "I can't leave her to that horrible bunyip."

The other people scoffed at this. "How are you going to do that? Likely you'll just end up as the bunyip's supper, too."

But the young man didn't listen to the others. He was resolved to do what he could to rescue his wife, assuming that she hadn't already been eaten.

In the morning, the young man thought about how he might catch the bunyip, or at least find out where it was hiding. He hit upon the idea of baiting it with a meal of frogs. The young man went to the billabong and caught several frogs, then tied them to a stick and stuck it in the water in the middle of the billabong. When the stick with the frogs was secure, the man went and hid himself and waited for the bunyip to appear. He waited and waited throughout the whole day, but the bunyip never came. When the sun set, the young man went back home to rest.

In the morning, the young man went back to the billabong and found that the stick was still there, but all the frogs he had tied to it were gone.

"The bunyip must have come after I left and taken all the frogs," he thought. "Maybe if I try again, it will come back while I'm waiting, and then I'll be able to find my wife."

So the young man caught more frogs, tied them to a stick, and hid himself. For the whole day he waited, but the bunyip never appeared. When the sun set, the young man went home to rest, and in the morning he went back to the billabong, where he found that the frogs had once again disappeared.

For many days, the young man baited his trap, and for many days, he found all the frogs had been taken, but he never once saw the bunyip. Finally there came a day when it rained. Everything was dark and damp and wet. The man had set his trap as usual and hid himself to wait. This time, his patience was rewarded. The bunyip came to the billabong to take its meal of frogs. And who should be accompanying the monster but the young man's wife! The young man nearly shouted for joy, but he restrained himself and instead stood up from his hiding place and threw a spear right at the bunyip. The young man's arm was strong and his aim was true, and the spear went right through the bunyip's middle. The bunyip staggered back, but it wasn't yet dead. It grabbed a frog that was swimming by and threw it at the man, hitting him in the eye and temporarily blinding him.

This didn't stop the young man. Taking aim as carefully as he could with his blurry vision, he sent his boomerang flying at the bunyip's head. So skillful was his throw that one end of the boomerang buried itself in one of the bunyip's eyes. The bunyip howled and turned to run away.

"Come with me!" the man shouted to his wife as the bunyip fled the billabong. "Come with me! I'll take you away from that monster!"

The young woman held out her arms to her husband and wept, but when the bunyip turned and ran, the woman followed it, weeping all the while. The bunyip had put her under a spell so that she had to go with it wherever it went, whether she wanted to or not.

The young man ran after his wife and the bunyip. This time it was easy to follow them. The bunyip made no effort to hide its trail, and there was no mistaking the young woman's footprints in the soft soil of the billabong. Soon the bunyip arrived at a gum tree and slithered up into the branches. The young woman stopped at the foot of the tree and stood there, unable to move, while the bunyip hid in the tree, its one baleful eye glaring out from amongst the branches.

Not long afterward, the young man arrived at the tree. He looked at his wife, who was standing frozen at the foot of the tree, and then he looked up into the branches to see the bunyip staring at him with its one, terrible eye. The young man stared back at the bunyip, but this was a fatal mistake. The young man found he couldn't look away and that he couldn't move. He, too, had been put under the bunyip's spell.

For many days, nothing changed. The man and the woman stood at the foot of the tree, yearning to touch one another but unable to move, while the bunyip stayed in the branches, staring out at the world with its single eye. Then one day came a terrible storm, with driving rain and howling wind. So strong was the wind that it toppled the gum tree, killing the bunyip. But the eye of the bunyip remained exactly where it was, and this is how the moon was made.

The death of the bunyip broke the spell on the young couple. They ran into each other's arms and embraced and wept with joy. They were united with the rest of their people and told them the whole tale. And from that day forth, the people of the Frog tribe never ate another frog. Instead, they leave them for the bunyip so that it will take the frogs instead of taking them.

The Adventures of Yooneeara

The Kamilaroi (Gamilaraay) people traditionally have lived in New South Wales and Queensland. They are among the Indigenous Australians who revere Baiame as a god and hero. In the myth retold below, a young man named Yooneeara decides to go and find Kurrilwan, the place where Baiame lives, at the end of the world where the sun sets. Yooneeara has many and varied adventures along the way, braving strange, not-quite-human people, stinging insects, and a dangerous swamp before arriving at his destination. Yooneeara reaches his goal and arrives home safely, but like all who venture into the places where the divine lays hidden, Yooneeara ultimately must pay a price for his journey by dying prematurely.

One day, Yooneeara of the Kamilaroi said, "I think I shall go to the place where the sun sets."

"What do you want to do that for?" asked the people of his camp. "It's a long way, and nobody who set out for that place has ever returned. You don't even know how to get there."

"Oh, I'm sure I'll figure out how to get there, and anyway, it's important. The place where the sun sets is where Baiame lives, and I intend to visit him, there in his home in Kurrilwan."

"Suit yourself," said the other people, but they all thought Yooneeara was slightly mad.

Yooneeara prepared for his journey. He took his best weapons with him and a dilly bag for carrying things he would need. Right before he set out, he caught a bandicoot and put it in the bag. Surely it wouldn't hurt to have something like that. He would need to eat eventually, and what if he came to a place where game was scarce?

Finally everything was ready. Yooneeara said goodbye to his family and friends and walked westward out of the camp. For many days Yooneeara walked through the bush. For the first few days, he was in country that was familiar to him, but not long after, he found himself crossing into territory that he had never been to before. It was exciting to be in a new place, although a little frightening as well, but Yooneeara was a brave man, and he kept on walking westward.

After many days, Yooneeara came to the country of the Dhinnabarrada, people who have the bodies and heads of people but the legs and feet of emus. A group of the Dhinnabarrada ran up to Yooneeara. They had never seen a human being before, and they were very curious indeed. All of them wanted to touch his human feet, but Yooneeara would not let them. He knew that if they touched his feet, he would turn into one of them. The Dhinnabarrada kept crowding around him, and although Yooneeara managed to dodge away from their exploring hands, he soon feared he would not be able to keep them from touching him. Then Yooneeara remembered the bandicoot in his dilly bag. He hadn't seen any bandicoots for some time; maybe there were none in this country, and if he showed one to the Dhinnabarrada, it might distract them long enough for him to get away.

Yooneeara took the bandicoot out of his bag and released it at the feet of the Dhinnabarrada. All of the strange emu-footed people were fascinated by this new creature, and when the bandicoot scurried off to find shelter, the Dhinnabarrada followed it. Once the Dhinnabarrada were in pursuit of the bandicoot, Yooneeara ran as fast as he could out of their land.

Yooneeara journeyed on, moving ever westward. Soon he came to a wide plain that was the home of the Dheeyabery people. Yooneeara had never seen people like these before. They looked like regular humans from the front, but when they turned around, their backs were round and smooth and featureless.

The Dheeyabery gathered around Yooneeara. They had never seen anyone like him before, either. They touched his body, especially his back, which they found fascinatingly different from their own. Yooneeara endured this for a time, since the Dheeyabery did not seem to wish him harm, but eventually he had to run away. The Dheeyabery had touched him so much that he began to fear that he might turn into one of them if he stayed any longer.

The strange people were very sad that Yooneeara ran away. He could hear their voices calling to him as he ran. "Stay with us! Be our friend!" they called, but Yooneeara knew he could not stay. He needed to keep going westward if he were ever to come to Kurrilwan, the home of Baiame.

Eventually, the plain that was the home of the strange round-backed people came to an end and gave way to a large, stagnant marsh. Yooneeara was not pleased at having to cross this sort of terrain, but it was the only way he could see to reach his goal. Already, as he stood at the edge of the marsh, he was beginning to be worried by mosquitoes and March flies, which buzzed in his ears and bit him all over his body.

Bravely, Yooneeara entered the marsh. With every step he took, the insects became more numerous, and their bites and buzzing more unbearable. Finally Yooneeara was so miserable that he seriously considered turning around and heading home. But then he saw a tree that had soft, pliable bark, and he had an idea. Yooneeara peeled the bark off the tree and wrapped it around his body. He stuffed the boughs of bushes into the ends around his ankles and wrists. He made a helmet for his head with two eyeholes for him to see through.

Thus armored against the attacks of insects, Yooneeara waded through the marsh.

It was a long, hot, dreary walk through the marsh. Yooneeara was very glad indeed to reach the other side. When he had walked far enough that he thought he had left the insects behind, he took off his improvised armor, but he did not throw it away. "This might come in useful on the way home," he thought, so Yooneeara carried it along with him until he arrived at a place where there was a deep, clear spring of fresh water. He put his bark armor into the water, thinking to keep it soft and pliable for him to use when he came back this way.

As Yooneeara stood up from putting the armor into the water, he heard small voices calling, "Where are you? Where are you?" Yooneeara looked around but couldn't see anyone. Suddenly, a silver fish landed at his feet. This was even more puzzling. Yooneeara had never met fish that jumped out of the water of their own accord.

Yooneeara knelt by the water and looked carefully into its depths. There he saw many tiny men walking on the bottom. It was they who were calling, "Where are you?" As Yooneeara watched, the men caught a silver fish. They threw the fish up through the water, where it broke the surface and landed at Yooneeara's feet. Yooneeara watched the little men for a while longer, and while he watched, they threw more fish onto the bank from time to time.

Yooneeara gathered up all the fish and put them in his dilly bag. "Thank you for the fish!" he called to the tiny men at the bottom of the spring. He was indeed grateful; the fish would make a fine dinner, and he was very hungry and tired at the end of a trying day. Besides, the fish would save time on his journey. He could cook and eat them and not have to spend any time hunting.

Ever westward Yooneeara traveled. After many more days, he came to the camp of two very old women called the Weebullabulla. They were roasting yams and lizards over a very small fire. There were no other people with the women. They lived alone and would not allow any men to enter their camp. Yooneeara gave them a wide berth and walked onward, hoping that soon his journey would come to an end.

On the other side of the land of the Weebullabulla was a great swamp called Kollioroogla. Yooneeara knew that this was the last trial he had to face before arriving at the land of Baiame. The swamp spread on and on, all the way to the horizon, where the sun was beginning to set. Yooneeara's heart fell. There was no way he could cross the swamp safely. He had already tested the ground by pushing his spear into it, and it had sunk so far into the mud that Yooneeara nearly hadn't been able to get it back out again.

Gathering his last scrap of courage, Yooneeara began to walk along the edge of the swamp, hoping to find some way across. Soon he came to a place where a tall tree had fallen. Its roots sat on the edge of the swamp where Yooneeara was, and its trunk seemed to stretch all the way to the other side. The trunk was slender, but Yooneeara thought it could bear his weight, and besides, this was the only possible way across to the land of Kurrilwan, which Yooneeara was sure was just beyond the other side of the swamp.

Yooneeara climbed up onto the tree trunk and walked lightly along it. It swayed a little beneath his weight, but it held fast, and soon Yooneeara reached the solid ground on the other side. He walked a little way forward and soon came across an enormous rock. Yooneeara walked around the rock and found that on one side it was hollowed out like a cave. In front of the hollow was Byallaburragan, one of the daughters of Baiame. Byallaburragan sat before a fire, on which she was roasting a snake.

"Welcome, traveler," said Byallaburragan. "Welcome to Kurrilwan, the home of Baiame. You have had a long and dangerous journey. Come and sit by my fire and have something to eat."

Yooneeara sat down, and Byallaburragan gave him some of the roasted snake to eat. It was the most delicious thing Yooneeara had ever tasted, and it satisfied his hunger like nothing else. Yooneeara looked about him and saw that Kurrilwan was indeed a beautiful place. There were streams of clear water full of fish, the air was full of the sound of birdsong, and the fields were full of game. It was more wonderful than he had ever imagined.

Finally Yooneeara found the courage to speak to Byallaburragan. "Is it true that Baiame is here?" he said.

"Yes, this is his dwelling," said Byallaburragan. "He sleeps within that cave. You may look upon him, but do not wake him!"

Yooneeara went to the mouth of the cave. Inside the cave was a giant, many times taller than the tallest man. His body was well made and painted with sacred designs, and his face was very beautiful. Yooneeara watched Baiame sleep for a while, then went back to the fireside where he laid down and slept a deep, refreshing sleep of his own.

When Yooneeara awoke, he thanked Byallaburragan for her hospitality and began the long journey back to his home. Retracing his steps, Yooneeara traveled through all the places he had visited on his way to the land of the sunset. After a very long journey, he finally arrived home, where he was welcomed with great joy by his friends and family. But Yooneeara never recovered from the hardships of his travels to Kurrilwan, and a short time after he returned home, he died. And thus it was that Yooneeara was the only man who ever went to the home of Baiame and returned alive, and no one has ever made the attempt since.

The Byama Brothers

This tale of murder, magic, and revenge functions in part as an origin story for the bullroarer. A bullroarer is a musical instrument made of a blade of wood or other hard substance that is tied to a length of cord or string. When the bullroarer is spun rapidly through the air, it makes a low humming sound. Bullroarers have been used by various cultures throughout the world for millennia, and are often considered to be sacred instruments whose use is restricted only to those who have been properly initiated.

Indigenous Australian tribes such as the Kamilaroi and the Kurnai, both from southeastern Australia, use the bullroarer as part of the initiation ceremonies for young men. For these tribes, as for many others, the bullroarer is used exclusively by the men of the tribe for sacred purposes only. Women may hear the sound of the bullroarer, but they are not allowed to see or handle the instruments, on pain of death.

Once there were two brothers named Byama. Each brother had a young son named Weerooimbrall. A day came when the brothers needed to go hunting, and their wives needed to go along. So the parents brought their children to a secluded, rocky place and left them there to await their return.

The brothers and their wives had thought the rocky place to be a very safe spot for their children. It was hidden from view, and there didn't seem to be any dangerous animals or insects about. However, the brothers had forgotten about Thorkook, a bad-tempered man who kept a pack of vicious dogs and who hated both the Byama brothers with all his heart. Thorkook discovered where the brothers had left their children and decided to get his revenge by setting his dogs on them. The dogs were fierce and savage, and it didn't take long for them to maul the children to death.

When the brothers and their wives returned to fetch their children, all they found were their mangled bodies. The parents all sent up a great wailing, and the other people of their camp wailed along with them in grief for the death of the two boys.

Now, it was clear to the Byama brothers that the children had been mauled by dogs, and there was only one pack of dogs that vicious nearby: Thorkook's pack. So the brothers turned themselves into kangaroos and went hopping over to the place where Thorkook and his dogs lived. The brothers hopped close enough to the camp that the pack of dogs would scent them and give chase, and soon the kangaroos were bounding across the bush with a baying pack of dogs snapping close behind.

The brothers had no fear of the dogs; they were bigger, stronger, and faster, and they had a plan to destroy each and every one of them. They would let one dog get close, and when it made a jump for one of the brothers, that brother would lash out with his sharp claws and rend the dog in two. The brothers kept up the chase in this way until each and every one of the dogs had been killed.

After the whole pack was dead, the brothers turned themselves back into men and went to deal with Thorkook himself. They went into his camp and killed him without mercy. When Thorkook was dead, the brothers turned him into a mopoke, a small, brown bird with bulging eyes that only goes about at night.

Avenging their sons gave the brothers a little peace, but it did nothing to assuage the grief of their wives. Day and night, they wailed and mourned for their murdered children. Nothing the brothers could do would soothe them, so they turned their wives into curlews. And to this day, when curlews cry during the night, it is the wailing of the two mothers who are still mourning their sons.

Sometime after the death of the two boys, one brother climbed into a tree, where he used his axe to cut out a white wood grub. As he chopped at the wood of the tree, one chip went flying through the air with such force that it made a low, whizzing sound. The other brother had been standing at the foot of the tree waiting, and as the chip flew by, he cried out, "That is the sound of our sons' voices! Our sons' voices sounded just like that!"

Both brothers found this very comforting, but they did not know what they could do to preserve that sound. After some discussion, they both decided that it would be best if they spent the rest of the day hunting and that each would go in a different direction to search for game. One brother took his boomerang and his spear and went out into the bush, but the other stayed behind, holding the chip of wood in his hands and thinking hard.

The brother who stayed behind took his knife and smoothed out the chip. He cut a hole in one end and tied a bit of string to it. Then he began to swing the chip around, making it go faster and faster until it started making a soft, low sound, the sound of the voices of the dead children. Byama then went to the tree and cut a larger piece of wood. He shaped it carefully, cut a hole in one end, and tied a length of cord onto the hole. When he swung this piece of wood, the sound it made was much louder. And thus it was that the first bullroarer was made.

When the brother who had gone hunting returned home, the other showed him the bullroarer he had made. Both brothers rejoiced to hear the sound of their sons' voices again, even though they knew the boys were both dead. The brothers decided that the bullroarer was to be a sacred thing that would be shown to boys and made to sound during their initiation ceremonies. But never must a girl or a woman ever see the bullroarer, although they are allowed to hear its voice, for the bullroarer is a thing sacred to boys and men, since it was made in memory of the boys who were killed by Thorkook's dogs.

Part III: Animal Tales

Boora the Pelican

Dreamtime animal tales usually take one of two forms: either the present shape of an animal is the result of the animal performing human behaviors, or else it is the result of actions that result in a human being turned into an animal. The story retold below is of the former variety. Boora the Pelican lives and behaves like a human being, although he has feathers like a bird. When he engages in the human tradition of painting himself with white pipe-clay before going to war, he inspires other pelicans to do the same because they think it looks particularly handsome. This results in an irrevocable change that gives pelicans the white and black feathers they have today.

A long time ago in the Dreamtime, there was no water anywhere. This was because the frog kept it all inside of him and refused to share it with anyone else. All the creatures became thirstier and thirstier, so finally they held a council to decide what to do.

After a long discussion, the animals decided that if the frog could be made to laugh, it was likely that all the water would come pouring out of him. The first creature to try was the kookaburra. The kookaburra danced and fluttered his wings and laughed and laughed, but the frog only blinked and turned his back. Then the platypus came and tried making jokes about its funny beak and funny tail, but the frog only sighed and closed its eyes.

Creature after creature attempted to make the frog laugh, but none succeeded. The frog's mouth stayed firmly closed and the water stayed firmly inside no matter what silly things the creatures did. This went on and on until the eel went before the frog and started writhing and wriggling around. The frog watched the eel intently and smiled. The eel continued wriggling, and finally the frog could stand it no longer. He opened his mouth and laughed and laughed, and all the water that was inside him came out in a great gushing wave. Unfortunately, there was so much water inside the frog that when it came out all at once it caused a great flood, and many animals and people drowned.

Now, at this time, there was a pelican named Boora. He was quite vain and thought himself the handsomest creature in the world. In those days, all pelicans had black feathers, and Boora thought his own were the glossiest of any pelican he had ever seen. Boora also was very proud of the canoe that he owned. Of course, he didn't need it at all for getting about since he could fly and swim just as well as any other seabird. But it was a thing that none of the other pelicans had, and this made Boora happy.

On the day after the great flood, Boora went out for a paddle in his canoe. As he floated along, he came across a small, muddy island. On the island was a big log, and on the log sat three men and a woman. They had managed to save themselves from the rising water by grabbing onto the log, but now they were stranded on the little island with nothing to eat and no way to get to a dry place where they could find food. The floodwaters still flowed swiftly, swirling and rushing around the banks of the island, making the people afraid to try to swim to the piece of land they could see off in the distance.

Boora saw the people sitting on the log and became curious. As he paddled closer, he noticed that the woman was very beautiful. "Oh, my!" thought the pelican. "If I rescue her, she will be so grateful that surely she will consent to be my wife. She is very beautiful indeed, and it will make all the other pelicans even more envious of me if I have a wife like that!"

Boora brought his canoe up to the bank of the island. "Greetings, people!" he said. "What are you doing sitting there on that log? Where are all your friends? Where are your families?"

"We are stranded here," said one of the men. "All our families and friends drowned in the flood. We managed to grab this log and float along on it, but now we're stuck on this island. We don't know how to get to a dry place where we can find food because the water is still flowing so swiftly."

"Oh, dear," said Boora. "That sounds like a very difficult situation. Maybe I could help you. I have this fine canoe here; I could take you to that bit of land over there if you like."

The people discussed the pelican's offer quietly, and in the end they agreed to go with him.

"I'm glad to help you," said Boora. "My canoe is only big enough for one passenger at a time, though." Then he pointed to one of the men and said, "I'll take you first." The man got into the canoe, and away the pelican paddled to the opposite shore.

"I'll take the other men one by one," thought the pelican, "and when I go back for the woman, I'll have her all to myself, and nobody will be able to do anything about it!"

Boora returned to the island, and when he had beached the canoe, the woman started to get in it. "Not yet!" said Boora. "I'll take him next."

Boora invited the second man to get into the canoe. The man boarded, and then the pelican paddled away. He left the man on the far shore where he had left the first one, then went back to the island.

Again the woman made to get inside the canoe, and again Boora said, "Not yet! I'll take him next." Boora invited the third man to get into the canoe, and when the man had boarded, the pelican paddled away.

By this time, the woman was beginning to feel suspicious. "I'm sure that pelican has some kind of plan," she thought. "I'd rather risk a swim, even with this fast current, than let him take me away."

The woman looked about and saw a log floating by on the current. It was about the same size as herself, so she pulled it up onto the island and wrapped it in her own clothing. Then the woman slipped into the water and began to swim toward the opposite shore, taking care to stay out of the pelican's sight.

When Boora returned to the small island, he saw what he thought was the woman lying on the ground. "Get up!" he said. "It's your turn to ride in my canoe!"

Nothing happened. Again Boora said, "Hey, wake up! I can take you now!"

Again there was no reply. Boora became angry. He kicked at what he thought was a sleeping woman, then yelped and hopped about with pain when his foot struck the hard wood of the log. When Boora kicked the log, the clothing fell off it, and he saw that he had been tricked. He looked toward the opposite shore and saw the men helping the woman out of the water.

Boora flew into a rage. "I will make them regret that! I'll go over there and kill all the men and take the woman for myself! How dare they play tricks on Boora!"

Boora got into his canoe and paddled swiftly home. He gathered a quantity of white pipe-clay and began smearing it all over his feathers, for that is the proper thing to do when one is going to pick a fight. But the other pelicans saw Boora doing this and said, "What is this? Pelicans aren't supposed to be white. We are black birds, and that's the way it should stay."

The whole flock flew over to Boora's house and drove him away from their camp, shouting, "Stop painting yourself white! What a horrible, rude thing to do! Pelicans are black, and that's the way it should stay!"

But some of the younger pelicans saw what Boora looked like with white and black feathers and thought this to be extremely fine. So they began smearing themselves with white pipe-clay, and this is why pelicans have both black and white feathers today.

How the Kangaroo Got Its Tail

In Dreamtime stories, the final form of an animal often results from one or more acts of violence. Here, the kangaroo gets its tail from a spear thrust, while the wombat gets its flat head from a blow with a rock.

This story not only explains the forms and living habits of kangaroos and wombats, but it also functions as a fable about the value of timely work. The fight that changes the shapes of each animal begins with a quarrel that results from the kangaroo's tendency to procrastinate and to do tasks other than the one that most urgently needs completion, while the wombat is more diligent.

A long time ago, when the world was new, Mirram the Kangaroo and Wareen the Wombat both looked like men. They walked about on two legs and went hunting and fishing like men do. They were very good friends, and they shared their food and their water with one another. Mirram was tall and thin, while Wareen was short and heavyset.

Besides their shapes, there was one other important difference between Mirram and Wareen. Wareen liked to build himself a shelter made of bark where he could sleep warm and dry. Mirram, however, preferred to sleep outdoors. He liked being able to watch the stars at night. Sleeping outdoors was a fine thing for him to do, but not always. He was quite comfortable next to his campfire when the weather was warm and dry, but during cold and rainy times, he shivered miserably.

One day, Mirram and Wareen came back from hunting. Mirram made a fire in his fire pit, where they cooked their meal. When it was ready, they ate together, chatting amiably about their day. Soon Wareen finished his meal. He stood up and stretched and looked about him.

"Looks like bad weather will be coming soon," he said. "You might want to build a hut of your own, Mirram. I'd start now if I were you. There's plenty of bark to be had in that stand of trees over there."

Mirram looked at the horizon. He saw the clouds and agreed that Wareen was right. But he said, "Oh, there's plenty of time yet. I don't think there's any need to start right this moment."

Wareen was annoyed that his friend refused such good advice, but he didn't say anything about it. Instead, he said, "Suit yourself," and then went into his hut, where he laid down a fire to light when it became too cold to go without one.

The day wore on, and Mirram busied himself with other things that needed doing instead of building the hut. "The storm probably won't be too bad," he said, "so even if I don't get around to making a hut, it will be just fine."

By the time night fell, a little rain had started to fall and the wind had picked up, but Mirram was so tired from all the work he had done that he couldn't bring himself to make his hut. "I'll be fine right here next to my fire. There's not much wind, and there's not much rain. I don't think I'll need a hut."

But Mirram couldn't have been more wrong. This was no ordinary drizzle; it was a big storm, with howling winds and sheets and sheets of icy rain. There was no way Mirram could keep his fire lit. He had nothing to keep the cold rain off his body and nothing to keep the wind from knifing into his skin. Mirram looked over at Wareen's cozy hut and thought, "Wareen was right. I should have built a hut. But maybe he'll let me have a little space in his if I promise to listen to him next time."

Hugging his arms around himself in an attempt to warm up and keep off the rain, Mirram scurried over to Wareen's hut and poked his head inside.

"Wareen, it's awfully cold and wet out here. Please let me in," he said.

"No," said Wareen in a grumpy, sleepy voice. "You couldn't be bothered to listen to me earlier, and now I can't be bothered to help you."

"Please, old friend, let me in. I'm so very, very cold and wet and miserable," said Mirram. "I admit it: you were right. I should have built a hut. I'll surely take your advice next time, but for now may I have a little space by your fire? Just that little space, right over there."

"What, that little space?" said Wareen. "You won't fit, and besides, you're going to just drip all over me."

With that, Wareen rolled over onto his side. When he did this, it created another space in a different part of the hut.

"What about this little space here?" said Mirram. "I swear I won't take up any more room than that, and I'll be very, very quiet. Just please let me in."

"No," said Wareen. "You like to sleep outside. You keep telling me that all the time. You were too lazy to take my advice and build your own hut, and that's not my fault. So go sleep outside, and leave me alone."

Mirram crawled back out into the rain. He stood up and clapped his arms around his body, trying to keep warm. He was so very, very angry at Wareen. "Some friend he is," Mirram muttered to himself. "He won't even give me the tiniest space to stay out of this freezing rain, and I even promised to listen to him next time." Mirram looked down at the ground and saw a large rock. He picked it up and hefted it in his hand, then he looked back at Wareen's hut. "I'll show him what happens when you don't treat your friends well."

Mirram went into Wareen's hut. Wareen rolled over and saw Mirram standing over him with the rock in his hand. "What on earth are you doing, Mirram?" said Wareen.

"Teaching you a lesson about hospitality," replied Mirram, as he brought the rock smashing down onto Wareen's forehead, making it quite flat. "There. You couldn't be bothered to share with me, and now everyone will know that because your head will be flat forever."

Mirram turned to leave the hut, but before he could get away, Wareen grabbed a spear and thrust it into Mirram's back. The point of the spear entered at the base of Mirram's spine, and the shaft of it trailed along behind him. "If I'm to suffer with a flat head," said Wareen, "then you can suffer with a long tail!"

And this is why wombats are short, round creatures with flat heads, while kangaroos are tall and thin with very long tails. It is also why wombats like to live in dens where they are snug and dry, but kangaroos only ever sleep under whatever weather the world brings, and why those two creatures are never friendly with one another.

The Rainbird

The dingo is a wild dog native to Australia. It is thought to have arrived in Australia from Asia around 3,500 years ago. Dingoes were integral to the lives of Indigenous Australians, working as hunting dogs, watchdogs, and pets, and according to a study by archaeologists Jane Balme and Susan O'Connor, they likely were integrated in to Indigenous life and culture relatively early on.

In this story, we see a perversion of the relationship between humans and dingoes. Both the cannibal woman Yirbaik-baik and her pack of dingoes live outside the boundaries of normal human society, not only because they live apart from other people but also because they have made human beings their primary source of food. The punishment for this crime is for Yirbaik-baik to turn into a rainbird and her pack of dingoes into venomous snakes.

Once there was an old woman named Yirbaik-baik. She did not live in a camp with other people, for long ago she had decided to go into the bush and live with the dingoes. She had hundreds of dingoes who hunted for her. Together, she and the dingoes ate very well, and what they all ate was human flesh. Yirbaik-baik would go out with her two smallest dingoes and would wander about the bush until they found a hunting party. Yirbaik-baik would say to the hunters, "I know where you can find many wallabies. Go over there to that ridge and wait. My dogs and I will drive them to you. Be ready!" Then the men would go to the ridge, but instead of sending her two small dingoes to round up wallabies, Yirbaik-baik would call her whole pack and send them to the ridge, where they would maul the poor hunters to death. When all the hunters had been killed, the dingoes would drag the bodies back to their camp, where Yirbaik-baik would cook and eat some of the men herself while giving the rest to her dogs.

After a time, the people began to notice that many of their hunters did not come back to the camp. Enough of the hunters had now disappeared that everyone became very concerned. The next time a party of hunters gathered to go out, they decided to divide into two groups. One would go out into the bush to hunt as if nothing was wrong, while the other group would hang back and hide so that they could watch what happened to the others. Out they went into the bush, one party behaving as though they were tracking animals, with the other hanging back and hiding in what cover was available.

Soon enough, the hunters in hiding saw an old woman accompanied by two small dingoes approach the other group of hunters. The woman and the hunters spoke for a while, then the old woman pointed to some place in the distance. The hunters moved off in the direction the old woman had indicated to them, but they did not get far before the old woman let out a cry and hundreds of dingoes came swarming seemingly from out of nowhere. The dingoes fell upon the hunters and mauled them until they were all dead. Then the old woman turned and walked away from the massacre, and the dingoes followed her, dragging the bodies along with them.

The hunters who had witnessed the carnage wept with sorrow and rage at what had happened. They went back to their camp and told everyone what had happened to their friends and kinsmen.

"We cannot let this woman live another day," said one man. "We cannot let her and her dingoes eat any more of our hunters. We need to find a way to stop her."

All of the people agreed that this was the thing to be done. A large party of hunters armed themselves well and went out to the place where the others had been killed. They followed the trail back to the old woman's camp, where they saw their dead friends' bodies in a pile and the old woman butchering one of them while the dingoes lazed about the camp. The hunters ran down into the old woman's camp, where they slaughtered her and every single one of her dingoes. As When the dingoes were killed, they turned into venomous snakes, which slithered away into the bush. The skulls of the dead hunters transformed into great white boulders, which stand in that place to this day. Yirbaik-baik herself turned into a small brown bird, which flew away, giving a cry as it went.

This is how the rainbird came to be, and when people hear its cry, they know rain will soon be coming.

How the Koala Lost His Tail

Koalas are tree-dwelling marsupials native to eastern Australia. Several Indigenous legends describe the koala as having a long, beautiful tail, whereas the animal humans know now has none, inspiring stories about where the koala's tail went.

Just as Kangaroo gains a tail in an act of violence in the story told above, the legend presented here explains how Koala lost his, again with an act of violence involving Kangaroo. This story also draws on the koala's tendency to sleep up to twenty hours a day as part of the characterization of that animal, who is drawn as lazy and deceitful.

Kangaroo and Koala were best friends. They did everything together and shared the same hut, and they were both very proud of their long, beautiful tails.

A time came when there had been no rain for some weeks, and the weather had been very hot. All of the water was drying up, and the animals and birds were dying, one by one. Kangaroo and Koala were luckier than most because there was a small pool of water near their hut. The water wasn't very good, but it was water, so the friends stayed where they were and hoped for rain.

After many days, Kangaroo and Koala had drunk the last of the water in the small pool. Although many times there had been thick clouds on the horizon, the rain never came.

"Kangaroo, I fear we will die if we don't get water soon, but I don't know where to look for any," said Koala.

"I have an idea," said Kangaroo, "but it's only something my mother told me when I was a little joey. I might not be remembering it correctly, so it might not work, and we will die anyhow."

"Let's hear it," said Koala. "We may as well die trying to save ourselves instead of sitting here and waiting for death to take us."

"Well, my mother said that if you go to a place where there is a river, sometimes if you dig a deep hole on the bank, it will fill with water, even if the river itself is dry."

Koala agreed that it was worth the attempt, and so the two friends set out to find a river.

"I remember there being a river over that way," said Kangaroo.

"Let's go," said Koala, and off they went.

The two friends set out to find the river. They walked and walked, and as they went along, they saw the bodies of creatures who had already died of thirst. It wasn't a very cheering sight, especially since both Koala and Kangaroo were already so thirsty themselves.

After what seemed like an eternity of trudging through the dry heat, Kangaroo said, "We're here. This is the river."

"What river?" said Koala. "There's nothing here at all!"

"Well, you can see the path the water would take if there were any water," said Kangaroo. "I think we should start digging here and see what happens."

"Oh, I am so very tired, Kangaroo," said Koala. "I'm just going to lie down and rest for a bit. Why don't you get started on the hole, since you're the one who knows about these things. I'll join you later."

"Very well," said Kangaroo, and he began to dig a hole on the riverbank.

Kangaroo dug and dug, and the soil was dry all the way down. He dug and dug some more, but still the soil wasn't even a little bit damp. He was very tired indeed, and had begun to despair of ever finding any water.

Kangaroo climbed out of the hole and went to where Koala was sleeping. "Koala, wake up," said Kangaroo. "I'm so tired, and there's still a lot of digging left to do. Can you go and take a turn while I rest?"

Koala opened one eye and moaned. "Oh, friend Kangaroo, please don't ask me to dig. I am suffering so. I think I may die soon. I know I will die if I try to do anything other than lie here and sleep."

Kangaroo felt very sorry for his friend. He sighed and went back to digging. He was very nearly ready to give up and go lie down to die with Koala when the texture of the soil suddenly changed. Instead of being dry and sandy, the soil was moist. Kangaroo found new strength with the hope the damp soil gave him. He continued to dig as fast as he could, and in a very short time, water began to bubble up underneath his paws. He dug a little bit more, and the water came faster. Soon Kangaroo could see that there was so much water that the hole would soon be full.

Kangaroo jumped out of the hole and went over to his friend. "Koala! I found water! Come and see!"

Now, Koala had only been pretending to be ill. When he heard his friend say that there was water, he jumped up and pushed Kangaroo aside. "Out of my way!" shouted Koala as he hurried over to the water hole.

Koala bent over the water and drank and drank. Kangaroo thought it very rude of his friend to treat him that way. He said, "Hey, Koala, I did all the work. Let me have a drink now!"

But Koala would not move out of the way. He did not care that his friend had worked so hard. All he wanted was to drink and drink until he was almost ready to burst.

Kangaroo asked Koala to move aside twice more, but Koala pretended not to hear. Finally Kangaroo had had enough of Koala's selfishness. He took out his knife and grasped the end of Koala's fine tail. Then he slashed at the tail just a few inches from the root.

Koala screamed in pain and rage. He whirled around to find Kangaroo holding up a sharp knife in one paw and his beautiful tail in the other and looking very angry indeed. Koala wisely ran away as fast as he could. Kangaroo watched Koala go, laughing all the while. Then he went to the water hole and drank his fill, remembering his mother and her wisdom that had saved him. But Koala's tail never did grow back, and that is why koalas today have no tails at all.

Weedah the Mockingbird

Many people will be familiar with the tendency of some bird species to imitate not only the songs of other species but of sounds created in their environment. Chainsaws, car alarms, and sirens are only a few of the sounds that these kinds of birds can mimic.

In this story, the main character is referred to as a mockingbird. However, actual mockingbirds are not found in Australia but rather live in various habitats throughout the New World. Australia instead is home to the lyrebird, the Australian magpie, and the satin bowerbird, all of which engage in vocal mimicry, often as part of courting rituals. Since it is unclear exactly which Australian songbird is intended as the main character of this story and since the bird's mimicry is its most important feature, I am continuing to use the name "mockingbird" in this story as a generic term.

Weedah the Mockingbird had one great talent: he could imitate any voice he heard, whether it were human or animal, and he liked using that talent to play tricks on others. Weedah also was greedy and selfish. He didn't want to share the land with other people. "I wish I were the only one living here," he said to himself, "and that I never had any neighbors."

One day, while Weedah was practicing different kinds of human sounds, he hit upon an idea. "If I build a little camp with many huts and put fires in front of them, I can use it as a trap. I can make sounds to lure the people here and then be rid of them, one by one. It will take time, but eventually I will get what I want. And it will be entertaining in the process."

Weedah put his plan into action. He created a camp of many huts. He lit fires in front of each hut to make it look like someone lived there, and built one large fire in the very center. Then Weedah began to make sounds. He made the sounds of babies crying and children laughing. He made the sounds of women singing and men calling to one another. He made the sounds of old people telling stories. Any kind of sound that one might hear in a camp, Weedah made, and the sounds were the bait for his trap.

Whenever someone passed near enough to the false camp to hear Weedah's sounds, they would go looking to see who had begun living there. They would enter the camp, and at Weedah's invitation, they would look into each of the huts. Finding them empty, they would ask Weedah, "Where are all the people?" Weedah would say, "There's no one here, just as you saw. I think you're hearing things." Then the person would argue about what they heard with Weedah, who kept denying that there had been any sounds at all. During the argument, Weedah would step up to the person, making them step backward. In this way, Weedah maneuvered them closer and closer to the big fire. As soon as the person was in the right spot, Weedah would give them a shove and send them toppling into the flames. In this way, Weedah began ridding the land of the other people who lived there, one by one.

Weedah baited his trap and killed his prey for a very long time. Finally, people began to notice that many of their fellows had gone missing, more than could be accounted for by misfortune or other normal events. One day, Mullyan the Eagle Hawk decided to find out what had been going on and put a stop to it. Mullyan went out and found the trails of the last person who had left the camp and not returned. Mullyan followed the trail until he arrived at Weedah's false camp.

Weedah heard Mullyan's approach and began making his sounds as he usually did. Mullyan went into the false camp and began looking for the people he thought were making the sounds, but all he found was Weedah.

"What is going on here, Weedah?" said Mullyan.

"What do you mean?"

"Where are all the people?"

"There's no one here but me, as you can see," said Weedah.

"But I heard babies and children, women and men. Where are they?"

"I don't know what you mean," said Weedah, as he began shepherding Mullyan closer to the fire.

Fortunately, Mullyan was a very clever man, as well as very strong and very brave. He saw right away what Weedah was doing. "I see how you've been killing everyone," thought Mullyan. "Soon I will give you a taste of your own medicine."

Mullyan kept asking questions and Weedah kept answering them, not realizing that the tables had turned.

"Stop playing games, Weedah," said Mullyan, as the two men drew very close to the big fire.

"The only games being played are the ones in your imagination, Mullyan," said Weedah.

"I think not!" cried Mullyan, as he seized Weedah and threw him bodily into the fire. "Your little plan is over, Weedah. No more killing."

Now, when Weedah went crashing into the flames, his head struck a large rock that was on the ground nearby, killing him instantly. When Mullyan saw that Weedah was dead, he turned to go back home and tell everyone what had happened, but suddenly he heard a sound like a clap of thunder behind him. Mullyan turned around and saw that Weedah's head had burst open, and out of the opening fluttered a bird. The bird flitted over to the branch of a tree and began to sing a song that belonged to a different bird. While Mullyan watched and listened, the bird imitated a panoply of sounds. Weedah had become a mockingbird indeed.

How the Turtle Got Its Shell

As we have seen in the preceding animal tales, transgression of one sort or another is a primary cause of changes that give animals their appearance or even their existence at all, and this story is no different. Wayamba's hubris in first stealing a woman from a neighboring tribe and then thinking he can take on her enraged relatives by himself results in his transformation into an actual turtle.

There is also a sort of chicken-and-egg problem here. In this story, turtles apparently already exist in some fashion, since there is a tribe of people who take the animal for their totem, but the shelled creature that we know has yet to be created through Wayamba's actions.

Wayamba the Turtle found himself in want of a wife. He looked for one among the women of his camp, but none of the Turtle tribe women were pleasing to him. "I will never find a wife at this rate," he grumbled. "I give up. I'm just going to go hunting."

Wayamba took his weapons and went out into the bush. On his way, he came across Oolah the Spiny Lizard, who was out digging yams with her yam stick. Oolah was from the neighboring Spiny Lizard camp, and Wayamba had never seen her before. But the moment he laid eyes on her, he was smitten. "That is the woman I want for a wife!" he thought to himself. "I shall take her back to my hut with me right this instant."

Wayamba crept up behind Oolah and grabbed her. "Don't scream!" he warned her. "I won't hurt you if you come with me. I need a wife, and I think you're just the woman for me. Now, come along."

Oolah had no choice but to go with Wayamba. He was much stronger than she, and besides, he had all kinds of weapons. Oolah followed Wayamba back to the Turtle camp calmly, but inside she was frightened and angry.

When Wayamba entered his camp with Oolah, the other Turtle people said, "Who is this woman? Isn't she of the Spiny Lizard tribe? Why is she here with you?"

"She is my wife," said Wayamba. "I found her digging for yams and brought her back with me. None of the Turtle women are pleasing to me, but I like this Spiny Lizard woman very much indeed."

"Oh, that was a very bad thing you did!" said the other Turtle people. "What if her people come to get her back? You shouldn't have brought her here without permission. If her people come to fight to get her back, we're not going to help you, because it was wrong of you to take her like that."

Wayamba replied, "No matter. I'm a better fighter than anyone else in this whole camp. It's the Spiny Lizard people who need to be afraid of me." Then Wayamba took Oolah into his hut, where they passed the night together.

In the morning, there was a great commotion in Wayamba's camp. Wayamba peeked out of the door of his hut and saw that a large group of Oolah's people had arrived. They were all big, strong men, and all very well armed.

"Where is our Oolah?" the Spiny Lizard men said. "Bring her out at once! Let the foolish man who took her come out and face us!"

The people of the Turtle camp made no move to engage the Spiny Lizard men or even speak to them, but Wayamba didn't care.

"Ha!" thought Wayamba. "Look at all of them there. They're no match for me. There might be more of them, but I'm much cleverer!"

Wayamba took two shields. He tied one to the front of his body and the other to the back. Then he went out of his hut and cried, "Hey, Spiny Lizard men! I'm the one that stole your Oolah. Come and fight me, if you dare!"

The Spiny Lizard men hurled their spears at Wayamba, but he just pulled his arms, legs, and head into the shelter of his shields, and so none of the spears touched him.

"Is that the best you can do?" said Wayamba. "Come on, try again! I dare you!"

Again the Spiny Lizard men hurled spears at Wayamba, and again he retreated inside the shields. When the shower of spears stopped, Wayamba taunted the Spiny Lizard men once more, but this was a mistake. The Spiny Lizard men realized that spears would be no use, so they took their clubs and went after Wayamba. They were only able to get in a few blows before Wayamba turned and ran toward the river.

Soon Wayamba reached the riverbank. He paused, caught between the running water and the group of enraged, armed men who were closing in behind him. When a few of the Spiny Lizard men caught up to Wayamba and began hitting him with their clubs, Wayamba dove into the water and was never seen again.

The Spiny Lizard men went back to the Turtle camp to fetch Oolah and bring her home. The Turtle people made no move to stop them.

"Where is Wayamba?" the Turtle people asked.

"We don't know," said the Spiny Lizard people. "He jumped into the river and didn't come back up again."

Wayamba the man was never seen again, but a few days after Oolah was rescued by her people, some of the Turtle tribe were fishing at the river. They saw a strange creature climb up onto the bank. It had a hard shell on top and another on the bottom, much like two shields, and when the people picked the creature up, it pulled its head and legs into its shell. "So that's what became of Wayamba!" said the people. And that is how the turtle got its shell.

How the Platypus Came to Be

The platypus is a creature unique to Australia. It is a warm-blooded mammal that secretes milk for its young but reproduces by laying eggs. With its duck bill, webbed feet, and thick fur, the platypus looks as though it had been cobbled together from the leftover parts of other animals.

The odd structure of the platypus also engaged the imagination of Indigenous Australians, who created a myth explaining that the platypus was made out of the union of a duck and a rakali. The rakali, or water rat, is a rodent native to Australia that lives along the banks of rivers and other bodies of fresh water. It has a thick, glossy coat and a heavy tail, although not quite as heavy as that of the platypus.

A flock of ducks lived at the edge of a large pond. It was a good place for ducks; the water was cool and fresh, and there was plenty of good food. For the most part, the ducks stayed together at one end of the pond. "Don't leave the flock!" parents would tell their ducklings. "Don't swim out too far! If you do, Mulloka the Water Devil will get you!"

The ducklings mostly heeded their parents' warnings and stayed close to the rest of the flock. But one duckling was particularly adventurous. Her mother was constantly having to go after her and bring her back to the nesting area. When the duckling grew up into a beautiful young duck, she kept that adventurous spirit. Off she'd go exploring, and all the rest of the flock would shake their heads and say, "This time surely Mulloka will get her," but every time, Duck came back.

One day, Duck decided to go on another exploration. She swam down to the other end of the pond. When she got there, she climbed up onto the grassy bank to rest. "Oh, it is so lovely and quiet here!" she thought. "The flock is always so noisy. Everyone is always talking all the time. Here I can sit in peace for a while, and then I'll go back home."

Unfortunately for Duck, the grassy spot she had chosen to rest on was above Rakali's den. Now, Rakali was very lonely. He longed for a wife to keep him company. When he heard Duck's footsteps on his roof, he picked up his spear and went to investigate. He saw Duck sitting there and immediately fell in love with her. "Here is a good wife for me!" thought Rakali. "I shall take her home this instant."

Rakali crept over to Duck so quietly that she didn't hear him at all. Suddenly Rakali sprang at Duck and grabbed her by the neck. No matter how Duck flapped her wings and struggled, she couldn't get free of Rakali's grip.

Rakali brandished his spear at Duck and said, "Now, now, let's not make a fuss. I want a wife, and you are the most beautiful creature I have ever seen. Come quietly with me down to my den, and I'm sure we'll be very happy together. You don't want to know what will happen if you don't agree to marry me."

Duck realized she had no choice but to go with Rakali. For a time, she lived with him as his wife, but every day she kept an eye out for opportunities to escape.

One day, Rakali lay down in the burrow and took a nap. Duck realized this was her best chance to get away from him. She crept out of the burrow as quietly as she could. Avoiding the part of the bank that lay over the burrow, Duck swam quickly back to the end of the pond where the flock lived.

"Oh, look, Duck's back!" cried one of the ducks of the flock.

"Hey, weren't you eaten by Mulloka?" asked another.

Everyone crowded around and welcomed Duck back, asking her all sorts of questions about where she had been and what she had done when she was away.

Not long after Duck's return, nesting season arrived. All the young ducks found private places along the edges of the pond, where they made their nests and laid their eggs. When the eggs finally hatched, all of the proud young mothers went down to the water with their broods quacking in a line behind them.

"Oh, look at all the beautiful, young ducklings!" the grown ducks would say. "Aren't they just the cutest little things?"

Then Duck went down to the pond with her brood. But no one told her that her ducklings were beautiful. And no one said they were cute. Duck's children had the beaks of ducks and the webbed feet of ducks, but where ducks have only two feet, these children had four. Their bodies looked like that of a rakali, and they were covered with soft, brown fur. They had wide, thick tails and little spurs on the tops of their back feet.

"What on earth are those?" said some of the flock when Duck brought her young ones down to the pond.

"You can't seriously be proud of those things. Those can't really be ducklings," said others.

Yet others grimaced and complained that the two small creatures were the ugliest things they had ever seen.

But Duck paid the flock no mind at all. These two little ones were her children no matter what they looked like, and she loved them like no others. She raised them well, and in time they went on to make their own homes and raise their own children, who looked just like their parents. And this is how the platypus came to be.

Check out another mythology book by Matt Clayton

Bibliography

n. a. "Indigenous Peoples and Cultures." *Australian Government*. https://www.australia.gov.au/about-australia/our-country/our-people. Accessed 3 January 2020.

Allen, Louis A. *Time Before Morning: Art and Myths of the Australian Aborigines*. New York: Thomas Y. Crowell Company, 1975.

Andrews, Munyah. *Sisters of the Pleiades: Stories from Around the World*. North Melbourne: Spinifex Press Pty. Ltd., 2004.

Australian Geographic Staff. "DNA Confirms Aboriginal Culture One of the Earth's Oldest." *Australian Geographic*, 23 September 2011. http://www.australiangeographic.com.au/journal/Aboriginal-Australians-the-oldest-culture-on-Earth.htm. Accessed 3 January 2020.

Balme, Jane, and Susan O'Connor. "Dingoes and Aboriginal Social Organization in Holocene Australia." *Journal of Archaeological Science* 7 (2016): 775-781.

Bruce, Mary Grant. *The Stone Axe of Burkamukk*. London: Ward, Lock & Co., 1922.

Dixon, Roland Burrage. *The Mythology of All Races*. Vol. 9. *Oceanic*. Boston: Marshall Jones Company, 1916.

Fison, Lorimer, and A. W. Howitt. *Kamilaroi and Kurnai*. Melbourne: G. Robinson, 1880.

Flood, Bo, Beret E. Strong, and William Flood. *Pacific Island Legends: Tales from Micronesia, Melanesia, Polynesia, and Australia*. Honolulu: The Bess Press, 1999.

Hadley, Eric, and Tessa Hadley. "Yhi Brings the Earth to Life." In *Mythic Voices*. Ed. Celia Barker Lottridge and Alison Dickie. Evanston: McDougal, Littell & Co., 1994.

Huizen, Jennifer. "Dingoes and Aboriginal Australians Have Likely Been Tight from the Start." *Animalogic* (25 October 2015). https://animalogic.c43esa/news/dingoes-and-aboriginal-australians-have-likely-been-tight-from-the-start. Accessed 5 January 2020.

Irfan, Umair, and Christina Animashaun. "Australia's Massive Fires, as Seen from Space." *Vox*. https://www.vox.com/2020/1/3/21048700/australia-fires-2019-map-satellite-smoke-pollution. Accessed 3 January 2020.

James, Diane. "*Tjukurpa* Time." In *Long History Deep Time: Deepening Histories of Place*. Ed. Ann McGrath and Mary Anne Jebb, pp. 33-45. Acton: Australian National University Press, 2015.

Marshall, James Vance. *Stories from the Billabong*. London: Frances Lincoln Ltd., 2008.

Massola, Aldo. *Bunjil's Cave: Myths, Legends and Superstitions of the Aborigines of South-East Australia*. Melbourne: Lansdowne Press, 1968.

Mathews, R. H. *Folklore of the Australian Aborigines*. Sydney: Hennessey, Harper and Company, 1899.

Monaghan, Patricia. *Encyclopedia of Goddesses & Heroines*. Revised ed. Novato: New World Library, 2014.

Mountford, Charles P. *The First Sunrise: Australian Aboriginal Myths*. Adelaide: Rigby, Ltd., 1971.

———. *Ayers Rock: Its People, Their Beliefs, and Their Art*. Honolulu: East-West Center Press, 1965.

———. *The Dreamtime: Australian Aboriginal Myths*. Adelaide: Rigby Limited, 1965.

Parker, K. Langloh. *More Australian Legendary Tales*. London: D. Nutt, 1898.

———. *Australian Legendary Tales: Folklore of the Noongaburrahs as told to the Piccaninnies*. London: D. Nutt, 1897.

Paul, Leslie. *Nature Into History*. London: Faber and Faber, Ltd., 1957.

Peck, C. W. *Australian Legends: Tales Handed Down from the Remotest Times by the Autocthonous Inhabitants of Our Land*. Sydney: Stafford, 1925.

Reed, Alexander Wyclif. *Aboriginal Myths: Tales of the Dreamtime*. Balgowlah: Reed Books Pty. Ltd., 1978.

———. *Myths and Legends of Australia*. New York: Taplinger Publishing Co., 1973.

———. *Aboriginal Fables and Legendary Tales*. Sydney: A. H. & A. W. Reed Pty., Ltd., 1965.

Roberts, Ainsley, and Charles P. Mountford. *The Dreamtime*. Adelaide: Rigby, Ltd., 1965.

Rose, Carol. *Giants, Monsters & Dragons: An Encyclopedia of Folklore, Legend, and Myth*. New York: W. W. Norton & Co., 2000.

Smith, W. Ramsay. *Myths & Legends of the Australian Aboriginals*. London: George G. Harrap & Co., Ltd., 1930.

Smyth, R. Brough. *The Aborigines of Victoria*. Melbourne: Ferres, 1878.

Taplin, George. "The Narrinyeri." In *Native Tribes of South Australia*, pp. 1-156. Adelaide: E. S. Wigg & Son, 1879.

Thomas, William Edward. *Some Myths and Legends of the Australian Aborigines*. Melbourne: Whitcombe & Tombs, 1923.

Watson, Irene. *Aboriginal Peoples, Colonialism and International Law*. Abingdon: Routledge, 2015.

Printed in Great Britain
by Amazon